Max Begley and
David Sadler

Letts Educational
Chiswick Centre
414 Chiswick High Road
London W4 5TF
Tel: 020 8996 3333
Fax: 020 8996 8390

First published 2004

Commissioned by Cassandra Birmingham

Editorial, cover and inside design and project management by DP Press Ltd., Kent.

British Library Cataloguing in Publication Data. A CIP record of this book is available from the British Library.

ISBN 1843153319

Letts Educational is a division of Granada Learning, part of Granada plc.

Acknowledgements
The author and publisher are grateful to the copyright holders for permission to use quoted materials and images.
Screen shots reprinted by permission from Microsoft Corporation.
Every effort has been made to obtain permission for the use of copyright material. The author and publisher will gladly receive information enabling them to rectify any error or omission in subsequent editions.

Printed in Italy

CONTENTS

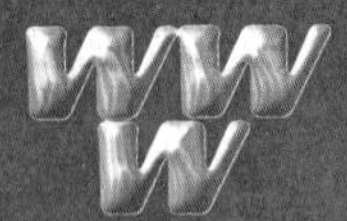

OPENING A BROWSER

SKILLS

.: Web browsers :.

To look at the world wide web you will need a web browser. The two most commonly used browsers are Internet Explorer and Netscape Navigator although there are others available.

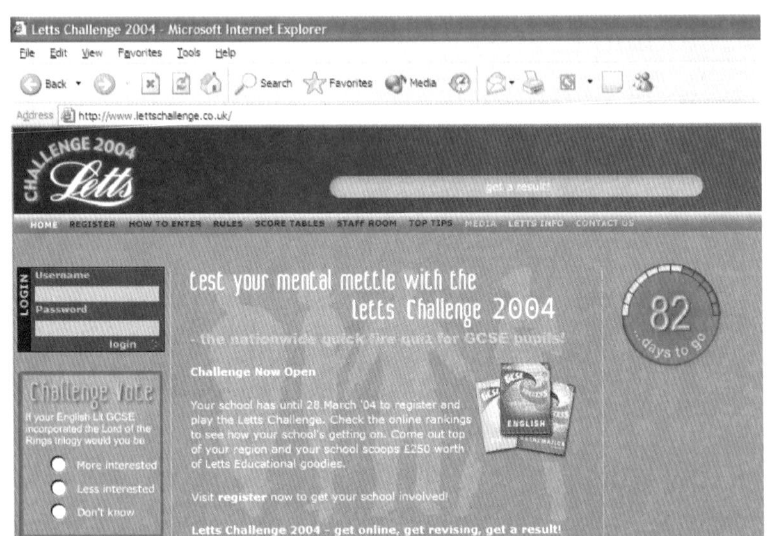

.: Uses of web browsers :.

You can use a web browser online or offline depending on what you are doing. The most common use of a web browser is for searching the internet. You might also use a browser for checking sites offline, previewing a website during construction or browsing an intranet.

.: Temporary internet files :.

You can save internet pages to your computer, although the sites you visit will be stored temporarily in a Windows folder.

Temporary Internet Files

PC MASTER TIP

If you have two or more pages open, you can switch between pages by holding down **Alt** while you click on **Tab**.

SKILL IN ACTION

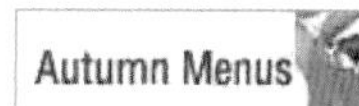

Cassie the Cook uses the internet every day. She looks up recipes, orders food and emails suppliers. Each morning she opens the web browser and does her daily tasks.

She leaves the web browser open because she has a broadband connection. This means she can check information quickly throughout the day.

At the end of the day she closes the web browser and shuts down the computer.

EXERCISE

Open and close a web browser.

SKILLS

.: How to open a web browser :.

There are several ways of opening your browser. You may have an icon on the desktop from your internet service provider (ISP), which when selected not only opens the browser but also connects you to the internet.

ISP icon

Web browser icon

.: Using broadband :.

With a broadband internet connection, you are automatically connected to the internet. The method of opening the browser is slightly different. You may have a web browser icon on the desktop. If so, double click the mouse on the icon and your browser will open.

.: How to open a web browser :.

If you do not have an icon on the desktop, click **Start**. You will see the icon at the top of the first column of options. By clicking on the browser icon, the browser will open to your home page.

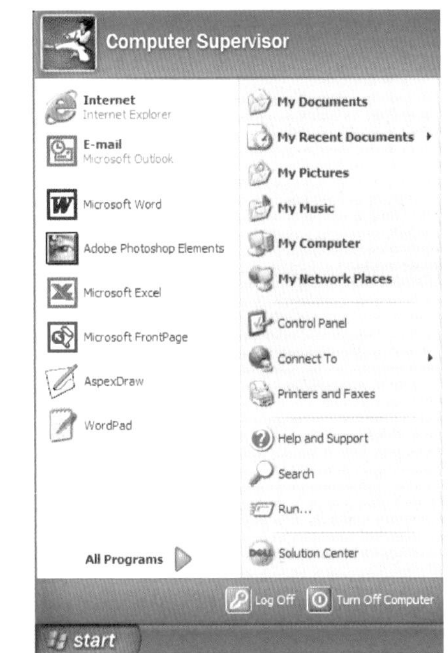

PC MASTER TIP

If you use the internet regularly, you can create icons for your desktop by right clicking on the desktop.

PROGRESS CHECK EXERCISE

Can you open and close a web browser?

Hint: Try using the **Start** button to find the browser.

Start button

Can you open two pages of web browser at the same time and use Alt + tab to flip between the two?

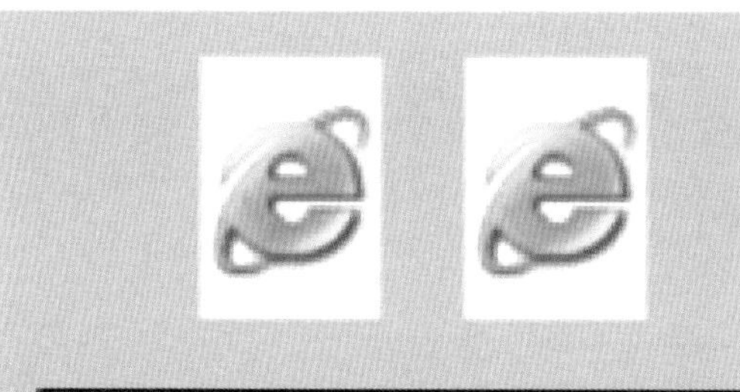

This screen appears to show that there are two internet pages open.

Can you minimise a browser so that it only shows in the task bar at the bottom of the page?

The Letts Educational website has been minimised in the image above.

MASTERCLASS

Can you save a web page in a folder as you would a normal file?

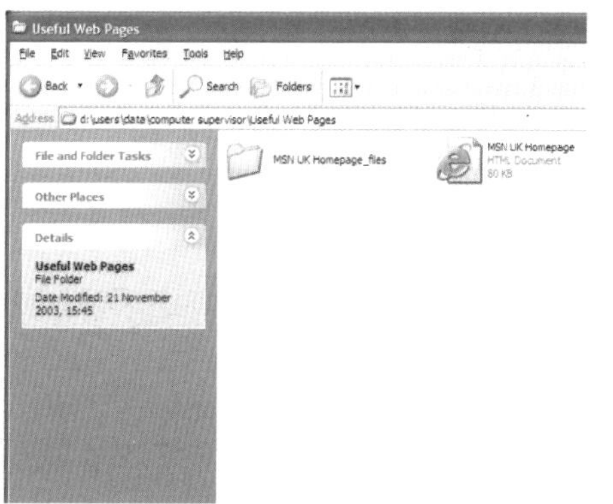

FINDING A WEB PAGE

0100101011010010100101110100101010111010101101110000101011

SKILLS

.: Search engines :.

A website can be found by many different methods. You can type a website address or URL if you know it, or you can use a search engine.

A search engine is a website specifically designed to find information and websites. Popular search engines are Yahoo, Google and MSN, although there are many more. Once on a search engine site, you can use key words to search for what you are looking for.

.: Using key words :.

Key words are the most important words in a sentence. For example, if you were asked 'Why did King William win the Battle of Hastings in 1066?' The key words are King, William, battle and Hastings. 1066 is not a key word as there has only been one Battle of Hastings.

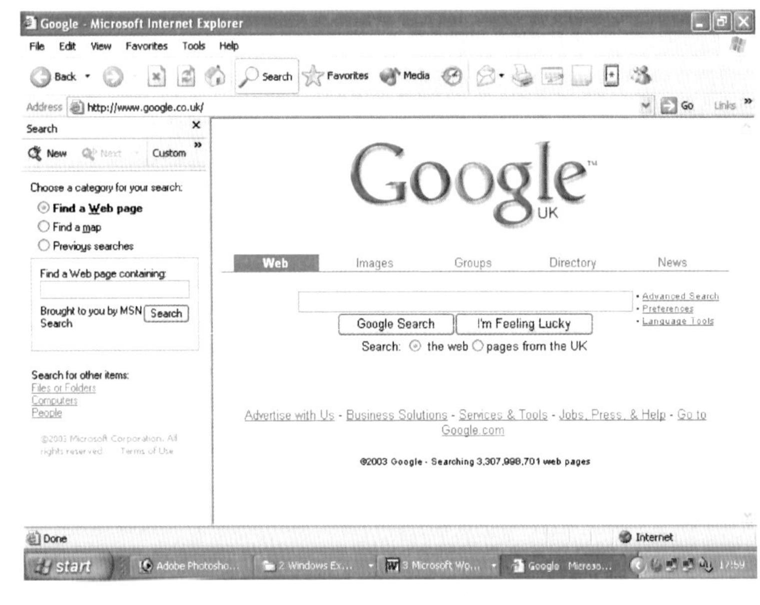

PC MASTER TIP

By using the correct key words it is usually easy to find the website that you need.

SKILL IN ACTION

Sophie the Student has to do a lot of research for her degree course. She uses books and papers from the university library and she also uses the internet.

While she is researching for some of her assignments, Sophie uses a search engine such as Yahoo or Google to find lots of different information.

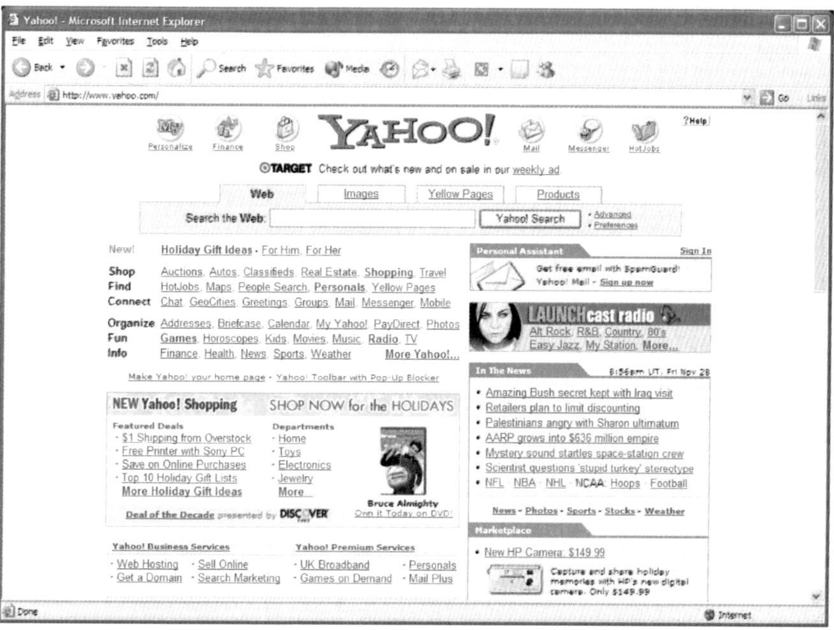

In some seminars and tutorials the lecturers suggest websites to visit for information. Sophie finds these easily once she gets on the internet.

EXERCISE

Find the Independent Television Company at www.itv.com.

SKILLS

.: Web address :.

If you already know the address of the website you want, you can simply type the address into the address bar at the top of the page.

The British Canoe Union - M

File Edit View Favorites Too

Back

Address

http://www.bcu.org.uk

.: Searching with key words :.

If you need to find a particular site, you can use a search engine. There are many search engines on the internet. If you are looking for a particular site but you do not know the address put in the key words for what you are looking for.

.: Searching with key words :.

If you do not know of a particular site and are just looking for any information or **surfing**, then you need to choose your key words carefully. For example, if you are looking for information about fighting in Normandy during the Second World War, you should pick out the key words 'Normandy' and 'WW2'. The search engine will give you a lot of suggestions and you should be able to find the information you want.

PC MASTER TIP

Remember that there is no guarantee that information you find on the internet is correct. Look at more than one source to check the reliability of the information.

PROGRESS CHECK EXERCISE

Can you type a web address into the address bar?

Can you type key words into a search engine and find a specific website?

Can you type key words into a search engine and find information on any given subject?

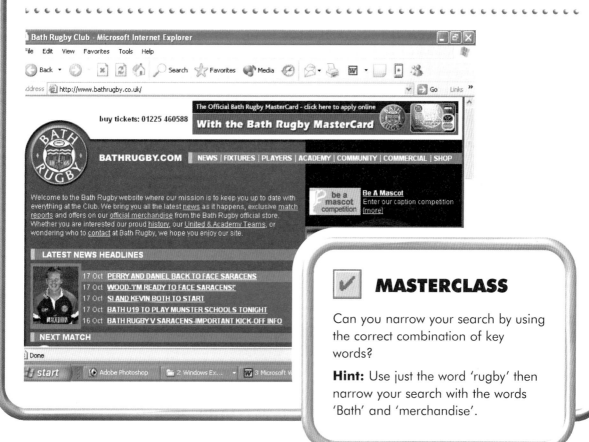

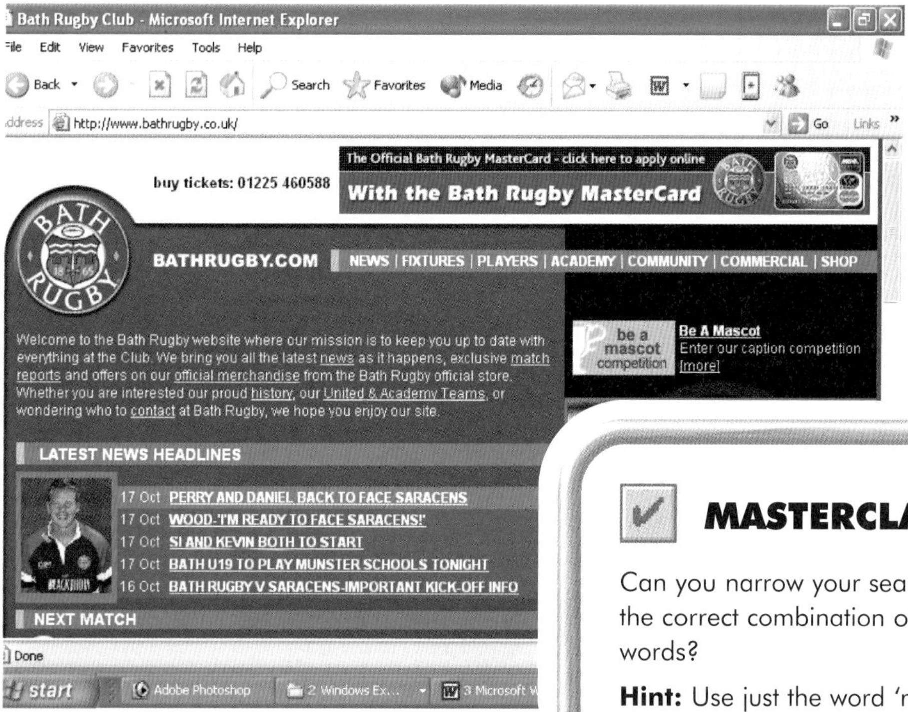

MASTERCLASS

Can you narrow your search by using the correct combination of key words?

Hint: Use just the word 'rugby' then narrow your search with the words 'Bath' and 'merchandise'.

COPY AND PASTE TEXT

SKILLS

.: Copying text :.

It is very useful to make copies of text from the internet and paste them into your own work. This saves time and helps to avoid typing errors.

You do need to remember to reference anything you copy so that everyone knows where it came from. You need to acknowledge the source of any material you use which is not yours. If you do not do this, you may be infringing copyright laws.

.: Copying :.

You can copy and paste in a number of ways. The copy and paste buttons on the toolbar, the Edit drop down menu, right clicking or shortcut keys can all be used to produce the same result.

PC MASTER TIP

You can use shortcuts for this. **Ctrl-A** is select all, **Ctrl-C** copies and **Ctrl-V** pastes. Just hold down **Ctrl** and press the relevant letter key.

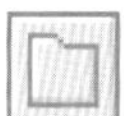

SKILL IN ACTION

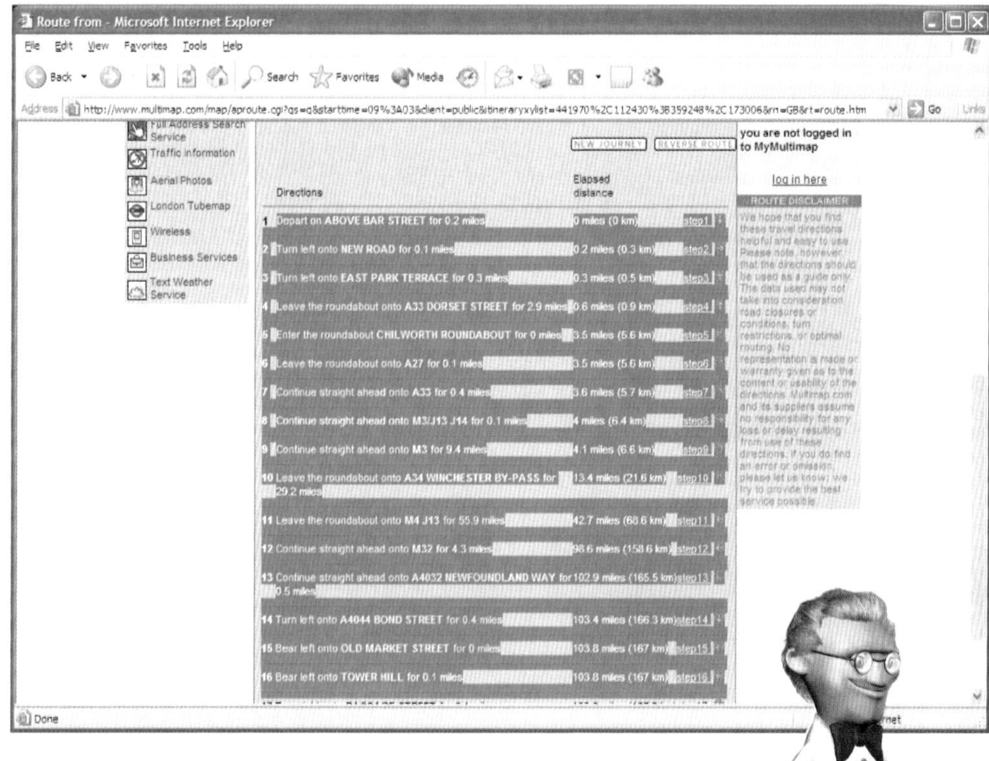

Harry the Hotelier uses copy and paste to save time setting up an advertisement for his golf course. He produced a website a year ago which has the directions to the hotel on it.

To save typing the directions out again, Harry launches a web browser, finds the hotel website and copies the directions from the website on to the advertisement he is making.

Using copy and paste, Harry can put the directions in to a word processing document. He can then send the document out to customers who are coming to the hotel.

EXERCISE

Can you copy and paste some text from a website into a word processing application?

SKILLS

.: Copying and pasting text :.

The basic process is to select the information, copy it and then paste it where you want it to go.

.: Selecting the information :.

Select the information from the internet by holding the mouse down as you drag over it. The text will appear with the colour reversed.

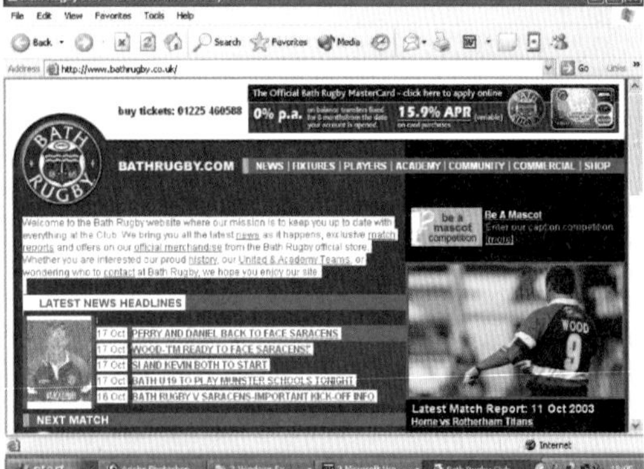

.: Copying the information :.

On the menu bar click **Edit** then **Copy.**

.: Pasting the information :.

Choose where you want the information to go, e.g. a document in Microsoft® Word. Put the cursor in the correct place and either click **Edit** then **Paste**, or click on the **paste** icon.

Paste icon 

PC MASTER TIP

It is usually better to copy and paste text and images separately because the computer is less likely to crash.

PROGRESS CHECK EXERCISE

Can you select just the text that you wish to copy?

Can you paste the text into another application and change it to look the same as the text already on the page?

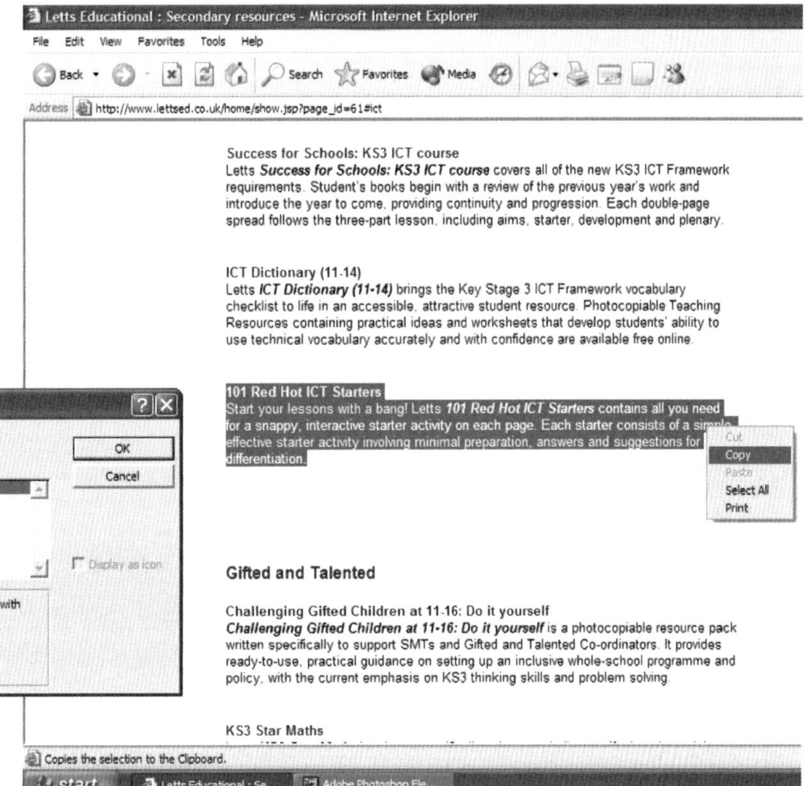

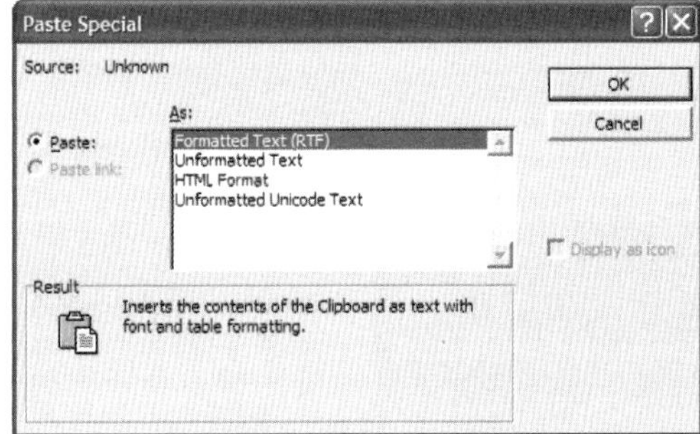

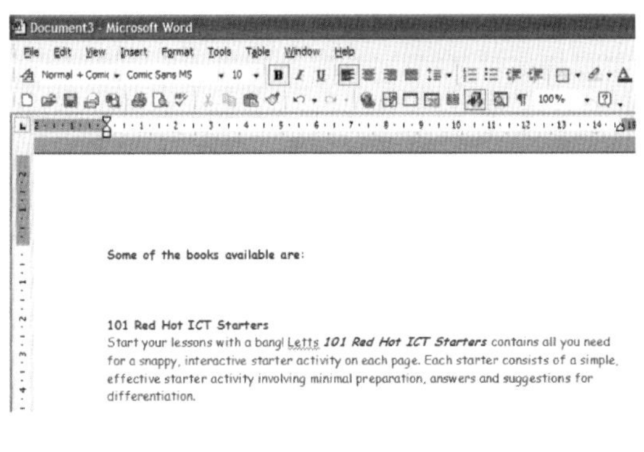

MASTERCLASS

Can you use the Paste Formatting menu effectively? Remember you do not always want to match the text you have pasted to your existing text.

COPY AND PASTE IMAGES

SKILLS

.: Copying images :.

It is very useful to make copies of pictures or graphics and paste them into your own work. This saves time taking a picture yourself or scanning one in from a book. You do need to remember to reference anything you copy so that everyone knows where it came from.

.: Copying images :.

Unlike text, you cannot always just highlight the picture and copy and paste it because it is a separate file. You need to use a pop-up menu, which you will see by right clicking the mouse on the image.

You can also save the picture to your computer using this menu.

PC MASTER TIP

Always make sure what you copy is correct so that you do not end up with any mistakes repeated in your own work.

SKILL IN ACTION

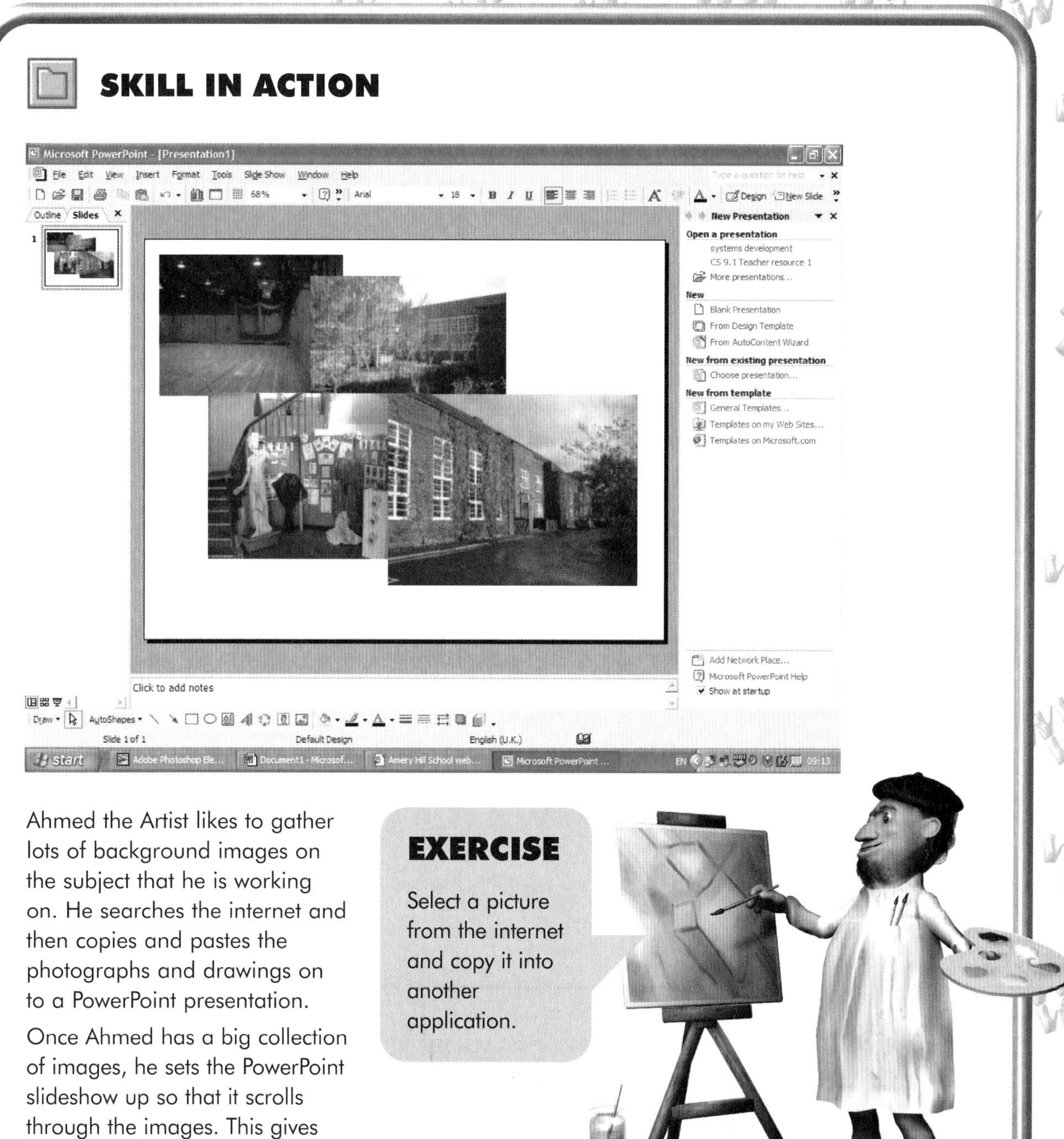

Ahmed the Artist likes to gather lots of background images on the subject that he is working on. He searches the internet and then copies and pastes the photographs and drawings on to a PowerPoint presentation.

Once Ahmed has a big collection of images, he sets the PowerPoint slideshow up so that it scrolls through the images. This gives him inspiration for his artwork.

EXERCISE

Select a picture from the internet and copy it into another application.

SKILLS

.: Select and copy :.

Left click to select the image, then copy the picture by selecting **Copy** from the **Edit** menu.

Edit Image Enhance Layer Select

Undo Select Canvas	Alt+Ctrl+Z
Step Forward	Ctrl+Y
Step Backward	Ctrl+Z
Cut	Ctrl+X
Copy	Ctrl+C
Copy Merged	Shft+Ctrl+C
Paste	Ctrl+V
Paste Into	Shft+Ctrl+V
Clear	
Duplicate Image...	

.: Open a new window :.

Open the program you want to paste the image into, e.g. Microsoft® PowerPoint.

.: Position :.

Choose where you want the picture to go. When you right click a drop down menu appears.

Open Link
Open Link in New Window
Save Target As...
Print Target
Show Picture
Save Picture As...
E-mail Picture...
Print Picture...
Go to My Pictures
Set as Background
Set as Desktop Item...
Cut
Copy
Copy Shortcut
Paste
Add to Favorites...
Properties

.: Paste :.

Either click **Edit** then **Paste** or click on the paste icon.

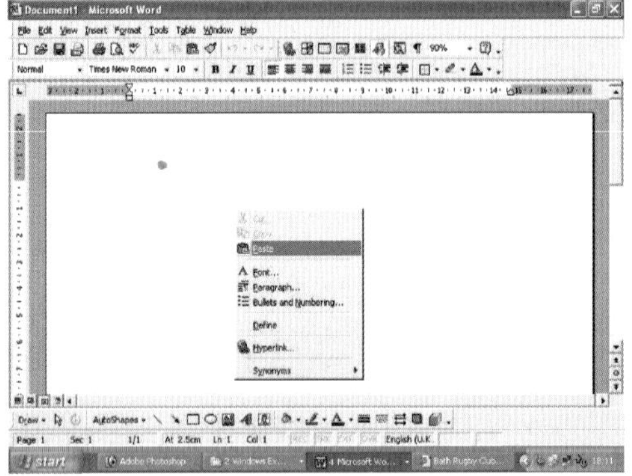

PC MASTER TIP

If you are having difficulty copying an image, you can insert it into the document from the **Insert** menu instead.

PROGRESS CHECK EXERCISE

Can you select a picture that you wish to copy and select Copy from the pop-up menu?

Can you paste the picture into another application?

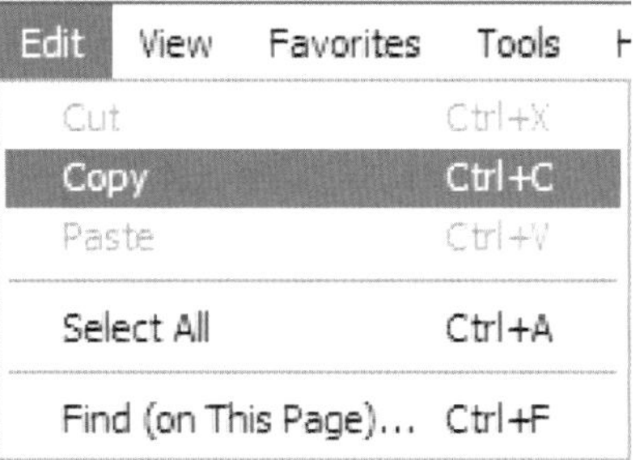

MASTERCLASS

Can you paste the picture into a photo editing application so that you can edit it before putting it into your work?

SKILLS

.: Converting table to text :.

Many websites are constructed using a table or frame that you cannot see once it is launched on to the internet. This makes placing the various graphics and text on the page a lot easier.

If you copy and paste the text from the website into Microsoft® Word, the table comes with it, making the text hard to edit.

1	Depart on **COLEBROOK STREET** for 0.2 miles	0 miles (0 km)	step1
2	Turn right onto **B3404 HIGH STREET** for 0.1 miles	0.2 miles (0.3 km)	step2
3	Turn left onto **ST JOHN'S STREET** for 0.2 miles	0.3 miles (0.4 km)	step3
4	Turn left onto **BLUE BALL HILL** for 0.1 miles	0.5 miles (0.7 km)	step4
5	Turn right onto **WATER LANE** for 0.1 miles	0.5 miles (0.8 km)	step5
6	Turn right onto **WALES STREET** for 0.2 miles	0.6 miles (0.9 km)	step6
7	Bear right onto **EASTON LANE** for 0.5 miles	0.8 miles (1.3 km)	step7
8	Leave the roundabout onto **A34 WINCHESTER BY-PASS** for 8.5 miles	1.3 miles (2.1 km)	step8
9	Continue straight ahead onto **A303** for 24 miles	9.8 miles (15.8 km)	step9
10	Enter the roundabout **LONGBARROW ROUNDABOUT** for 0 miles	33.8 miles (54.3 km)	step10
11	Leave the roundabout onto **A303** for 6.7 miles	33.8 miles (54.4 km)	step11
12	Bear left onto **A36** for 7 miles	40.5 miles (65.2 km)	step12
13	Enter the roundabout **COTLEY HIL ROUNDABOUT** for 0 miles	47.5 miles (76.5 km)	step13
14	Leave the roundabout onto **A36** for 4.5 miles	47.5 miles (76.5 km)	step14
15	Enter the roundabout **CLEY HILL ROUNDABOUT** for 0 miles	52.1 miles (83.8 km)	step15
16	Leave the roundabout onto **A362** for 0.6 miles	52.1 miles (83.8 km)	step16
17	Enter the roundabout **PICKET POST ROUNDABOUT**	52.7 miles (84.7	step17

.: Converting table to text :.

To edit the text properly so that it fits into your work, you will have to get rid of the table and format the text to look the same as your own.

1 **STREET** for 0.2 miles	Depart on **COLEBROOK** 0 miles (0 km) step1
2 **HIGH STREET** for 0.1 miles	Turn right onto **B3404** 0.2 miles (0.3 km) step2
3 **STREET** for 0.2 miles	Turn left onto **ST JOHN'S** 0.3 miles (0.4 km) step3
4 **HILL** for 0.1 miles	Turn left onto **BLUE BALL** 0.5 miles (0.7 km) step4
5 **LANE** for 0.1 miles	Turn right onto **WATER** 0.5 miles (0.8 km) step5
6 **STREET** for 0.2 miles	Turn right onto **WALES** 0.6 miles (0.9 km) step6
7 **LANE** for 0.5 miles	Bear right onto **EASTON** 0.8 miles (1.3 km) step7
8 **A34 WINCHESTER BY-PASS** for 8.5 miles	Leave the roundabout onto 1.3 miles (2.1 km) step8
9 **A303** for 24 miles step9	Continue straight ahead onto 9.8 miles (15.8 km)
10 **LONGBARROW ROUNDABOUT** for 0 miles step10	Enter the roundabout 33.8 miles (54.3 km)
11 **A303** for 6.7 miles step11	Leave the roundabout onto 33.8 miles (54.4 km)
12 miles step12	Bear left onto **A36** for 7 40.5 miles (65.2 km)
13 **COTLEY HIL ROUNDABOUT** for 0 miles step13	Enter the roundabout 47.5 miles (76.5 km)
14 **A36** for 4.5 miles step14	Leave the roundabout onto 47.5 miles (76.5 km)
15 **HILL ROUNDABOUT** for 0 miles step15	Enter the roundabout **CLEY** 52.1 miles (83.8 km)
16 **A362** for 0.6 miles step16	Leave the roundabout onto 52.1 miles (83.8 km)

PC MASTER TIP

Most websites are written in tables, whether you can see the gridlines or not. If your text is not behaving the way it should, use the **table** button on the toolbar and check that the text is not divided into cells in a table.

SKILL IN ACTION

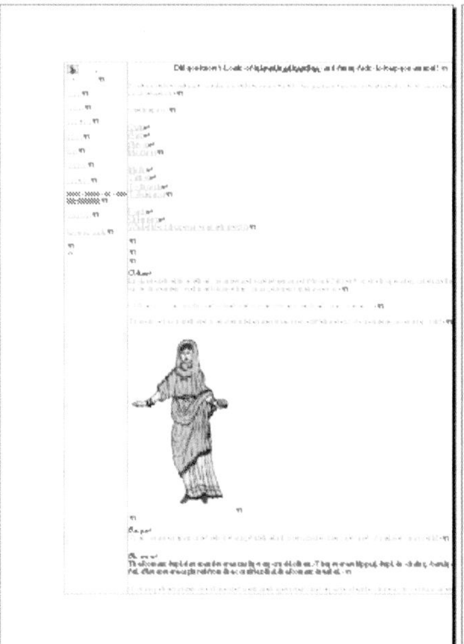

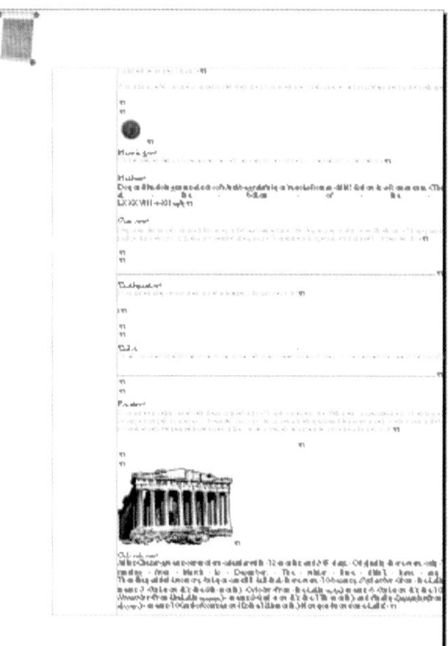

Sophie the Student often copies research material from the internet into her assignment to justify her conclusions. Much of the text she copies has been put in tables during the construction of the websites.

Sophie copies the text she needs from the internet and gets rid of the table layout so that she can format the text as she wants it. This information was copied from the internet and pasted into Word. The format looks odd because it is in tables.

Sophie notices that not all text has a table framing. This saves her having to delete the table every time she has to copy some text.

Sophie is always careful to acknowledge other people's material.

EXERCISE

Find some text on the internet, copy and paste it into Word. See if it is framed in a table.

SKILLS

.: Copy and paste web text :.

Select some text on a website. This could also include some graphics. Copy and paste the text from the internet browser into Word.

.: Selecting table text :.

Now select all the text within the table. Make sure that you do not select anything outside the table's borders or the next step will not work.

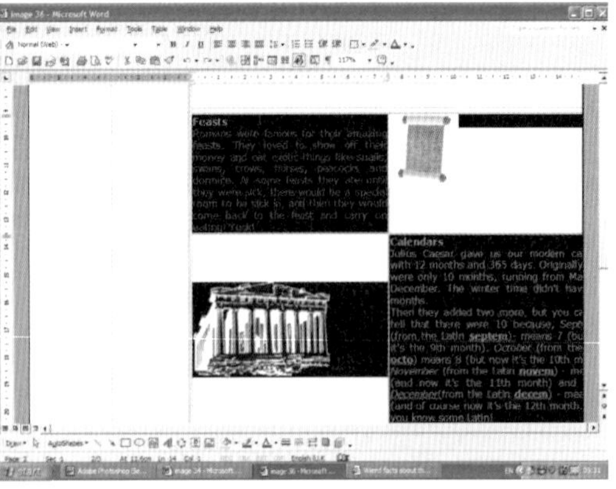

.: Removing the table :.

In the top menu bar, choose **Table** and then **Convert**. If you have selected the text correctly, you should now be able to select **Table to Text** and the table will disappear.

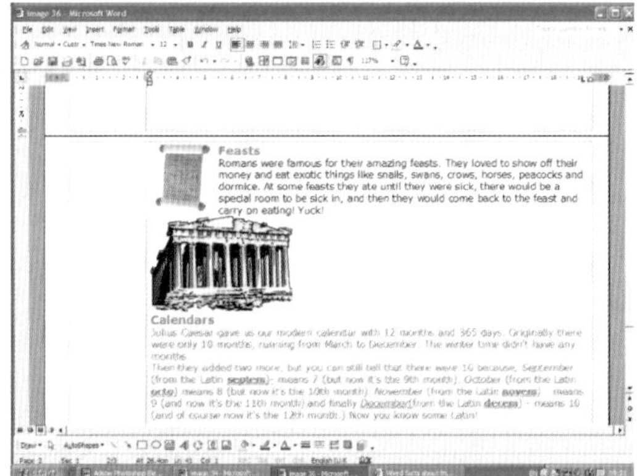

Feasts

Romans were famous for their amazing feasts. They loved to show off their money and eat exotic things like snails, swans, crows, horses, peacocks and dormice. At some feasts they ate until they were sick, there would be a special room to be sick in, and then they would come back to the feast and carry on eating! Yuck!

Calendars

Julius Caesar gave us our modern calendar with 12 months and 365 days. Originally there were only 10 months, running from March to December. The winter time didn't have any months.

Then they added two more, but you can still tell that there were 10 because, September (from the Latin septem)- means 7 (but now it's the 9th month). October (from the Latin octo) means 8 (but now it's the 10th month). November (from the Latin novem) - means 9 (and now it's the 11th month) and finally December(from the Latin decem) - means 10 (and of course now it's the 12th month.) Now you know some Latin!

.: Problem solving :.

If you cannot select the **Table to Text** option, go back and select the text again, making sure that you do not select anything outside the table frame.

PC MASTER TIP

You can convert the text back into a table once you have edited it.

PROGRESS CHECK EXERCISE

Can you remember how to select, copy and paste a piece of text from the internet into another application?

Can you then select all the text within the table you have copied?

Can you convert the table to text?

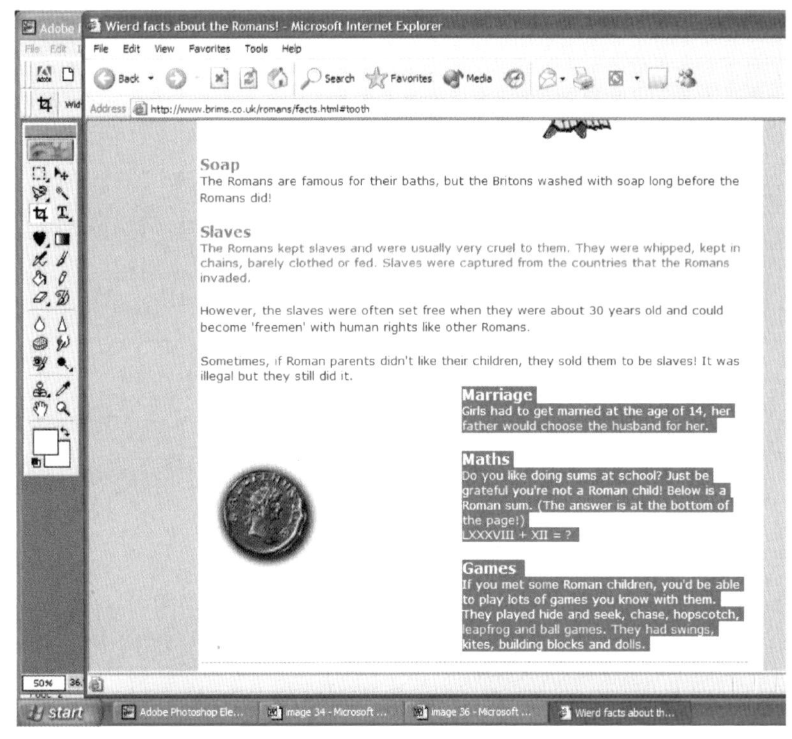

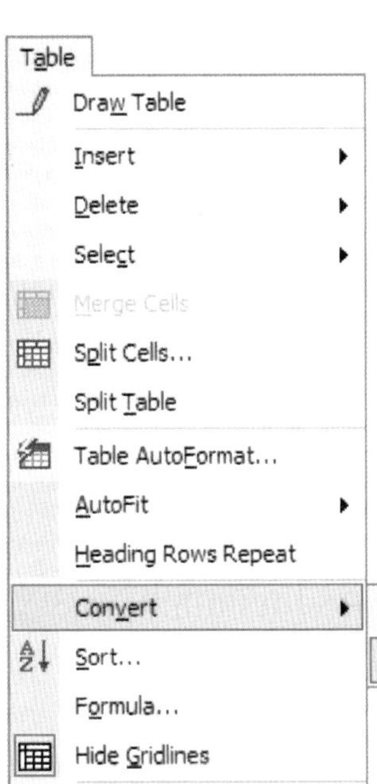

MASTERCLASS

Can you select pieces of text from the internet within a frame then copy and paste the text without copying the frame?

SKILLS

.: Creating simple web pages :.

Sometimes it is useful to store your documents as web pages. Many applications have the facility to create web pages. It is very simple to create a page in Microsoft® Word. In a few minutes it is possible to build the structure of a professional-looking website.

.: Starting a web document :.

When you open Word, a task pane should appear on the right-hand side of the screen. If it does not appear, you can show it by clicking on **View** and **Task Pane**. You can then click on **Blank Web Page** to begin a web page. The task pane is shown below.

.: Web Page wizard :.

Having your documents as web pages means that you can link them together, launch them on to the internet or create an intranet across a network.

You can use the Web Page wizard to help you create your web page.

Web Page wizard icon

PC MASTER TIP

After creating several documents you can link them together with buttons or hyperlinks, referencing different parts of the text to a glossary or picture.

SKILL IN ACTION

Kate's Kitchens

Projects 10-14

Projects 15-19

Projects 20-24

Latest Projects

Contact Me

Place an order

Order a catalogue

Kate the Kitchen Designer has created a basic website in Word showing her new kitchen designs. She does not want to put it on the internet yet.

Using Word, Kate produces several pages which show all her designs. She has a start or home page and an index page that contains links to all the other pages on her site.

EXERCISE

Create a simple start or home page using Microsoft® Word.

SKILLS

.: Creating a web page in Word :.

There are two ways of creating a website using Word. In both cases you need to open a new document through the File menu or task pane.

New

- Blank Document
- Blank Web Page
- Blank E-mail Message

.: Using a web wizard :.

If you want to start a wizard to help you, choose the **General Templates** option and then choose the **Web Pages** tab at the top of the window. This gives you several layout options and a wizard.

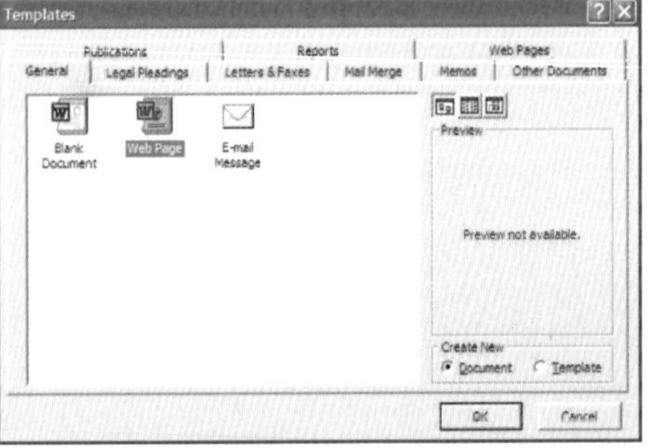

.: Using a web wizard :.

The wizard takes you through each step asking you to key in information which it will place on the page for you. When the wizard has finished, you can edit the web page yourself.

.: Creating a web page in Word :.

If you want to produce the whole page yourself, choose **New** from the **File** menu and then **Blank Web Page** on the right-hand side. This will open a new blank web page that you can fill in in any way you like.

You can type on the page or use text boxes and word art. Many web designers choose to create a table with three columns and several rows to assist them with the layout.

When you have finished or want to test your web page, choose **Web Page Preview** in the **File** drop down menu.

PC MASTER TIP

Any Word document can be saved as an HTML file, you do not always need to start one from scratch.

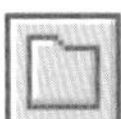

PROGRESS CHECK EXERCISE

Can you find and use the Web Page wizard?

Web Page

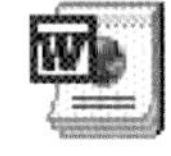

Can you start a web page from scratch and create a table to help you with the layout?

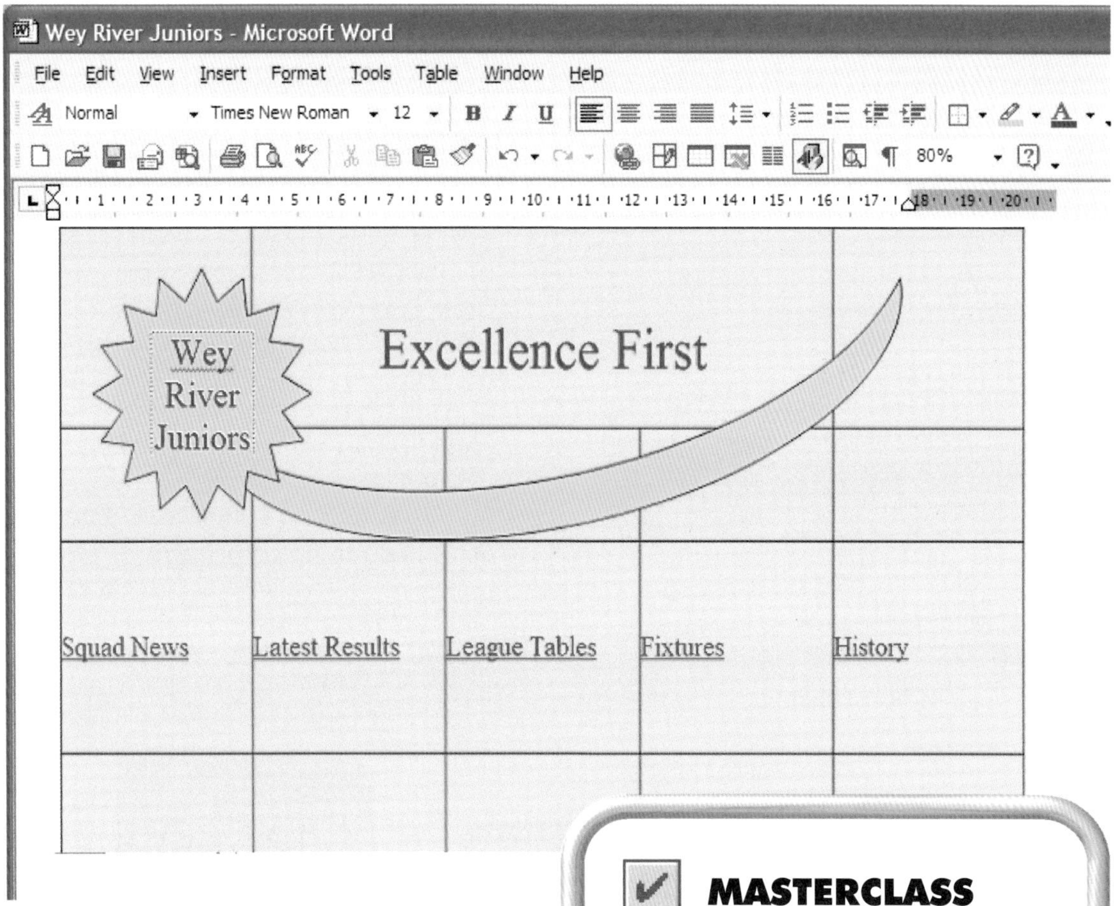

Wey River Juniors - Microsoft Word
File Edit View Insert Format Tools Table Window Help
Normal
Times New Roman
12
80%
Wey River Juniors
Excellence First
Squad News
Latest Results
League Tables
Fixtures
History

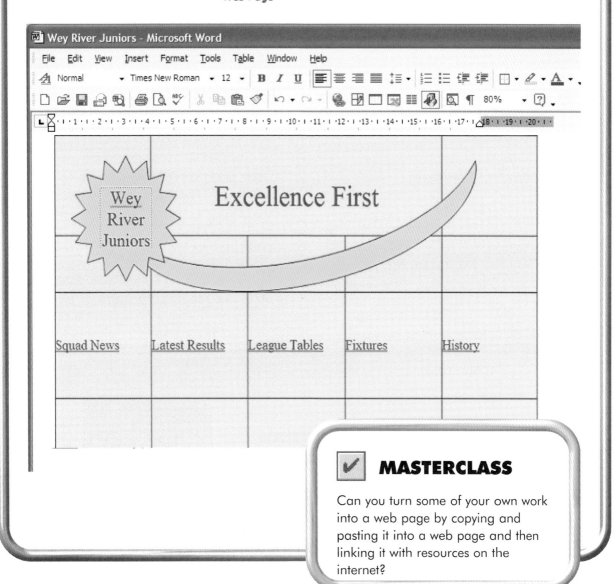

MASTERCLASS

Can you turn some of your own work into a web page by copying and pasting it into a web page and then linking it with resources on the internet?

01001010110100101001011101001010101110101011011100001010 11

SKILLS

.: Hyperlinks :.

It is very useful to be able to flick from one place on a page to another without having to scroll up or down, especially in a large document. If you need to reference a note or a definition, a hyperlink can be set up to take the reader to exactly the right place. You can use the **Back** icon to go back to where you were originally.

Click here for order form

Click here for calendar of events

Click here for times available

Click here for details of shows

.: Types of hyperlink :.

A hyperlink can be text, a picture or any graphic. Some websites have tiny hyperlinks so that they are like a secret entrance to part of the website. These are called 'Easter eggs'. A hyperlink is set up to link with another page or another place on the same page. A good hyperlink will tell you where it is taking you.

Click here to go back to top

Click here to jump to paragraph 2

Click here to scroll down to answers

Click here to go to bottom of page

PC MASTER TIP

Always make sure there is a hyperlink to take you back to the start if you are creating a website or intranet. This will help users not to get too lost.

SKILL IN ACTION

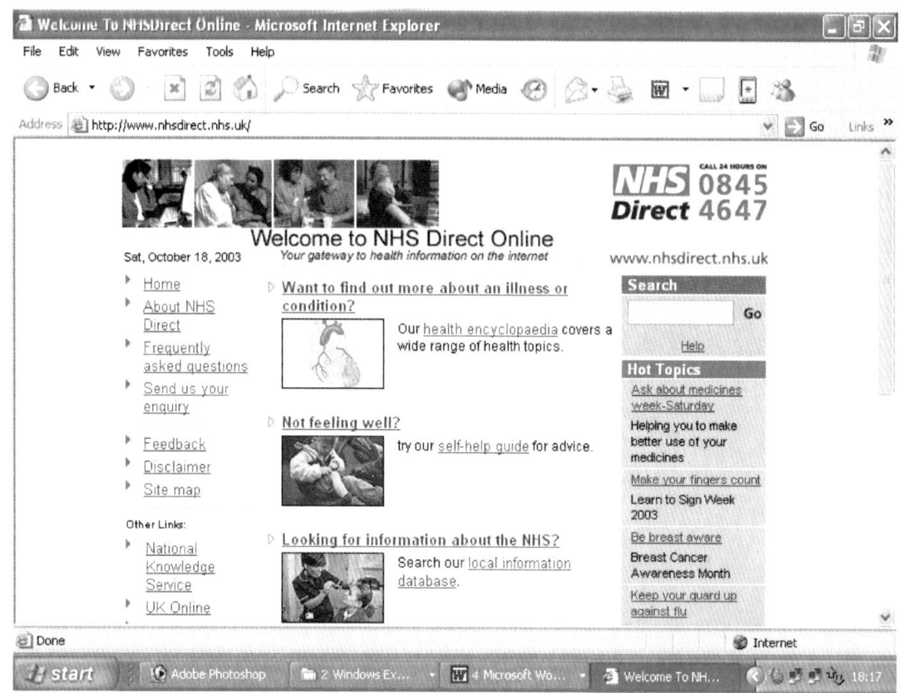

When Donald the Doctor is writing up his patients' notes on the computer he sometimes wants to link a sentence or word to something else. In the past he would put a star by it and then put a note in the margin. Now Donald can create hyperlinks to other parts of the notes or to a site on the internet such as the NHS website.

This saves Donald having to read back through lots of notes. He can just click on the link which takes him to the information he needs.

It also lets Donald tell his patients exactly where to look on the internet so they can find out more about their illness.

EXERCISE

Select a piece of text and create a hyperlink to a website.

SKILLS

.: The hyperlink icon :.

The hyperlink icon is in the top toolbar. To make a hyperlink, select the item that you wish to make into a hyperlink, then press the icon.

Hyperlink icon

.: The hyperlink window :.

Decide where you want the link to go, e.g. a website, another place in the document, a new document or an email address. Select the option you want and key the information into the correct field. Then click **OK** and the hyperlink will work.

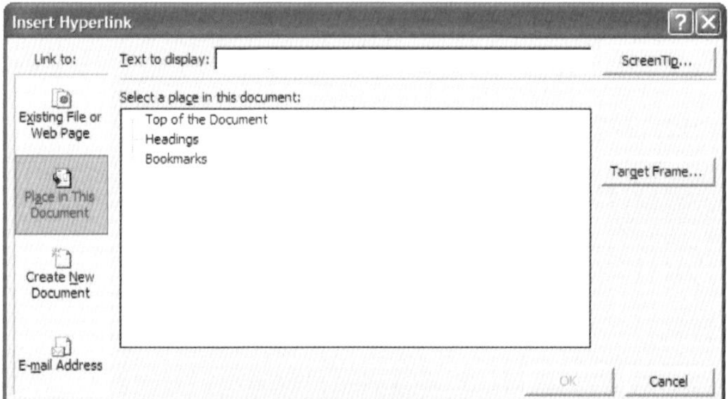

.: Using a hyperlink :.

On a normal page, you will have to press **Ctrl** and click the mouse to work the hyperlink. On a web page you can just click on the hyperlink.

.: Removing a hyperlink :.

To remove a hyperlink, highlight the link then press the **hyperlink** icon and press the **Remove Link** button in the bottom right corner of the window.

PC MASTER TIP

Some people put all the websites they use on to one page as a series of hyperlinks. This saves them having to remember website addresses.

PROGRESS CHECK EXERCISE

Can you set up a hyperlink to take you to each of the options in the hyperlink window?

Hint: You will need to have created the place you want to link to before setting up the hyperlink. This is easy to do for a website or a file. However, if you want to create a bookmark, you need to click on Insert, then Bookmark.

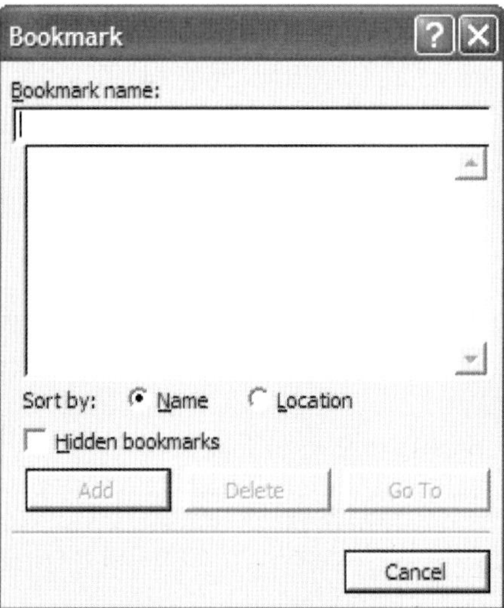

Can you select an object or piece of text to use as a hyperlink?

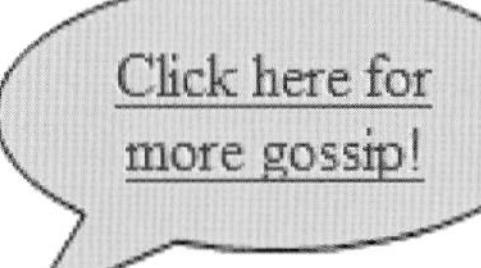

Can you remove a hyperlink from a document?

Hint: You will need to right click on the hyperlink to get the following menu:

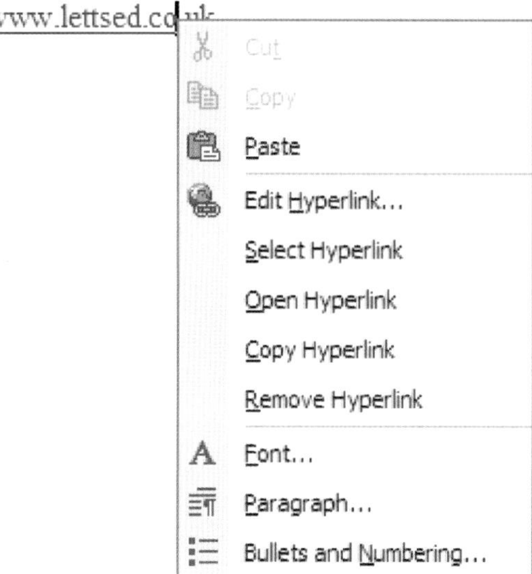

MASTERCLASS

Can you copy and paste a piece of text from the internet into your work and then delete all the hyperlinks from it?

SKILLS

.: Favorites :.

If you use the internet every day, it is useful to save a collection of sites that you use a lot. These can be stored in a tool called **Favorites**. There is an icon on the web browser's toolbar to help you do this.

Favorites

.: Using Favorites :.

Favorites stores the website addresses or URLs with a label on each so that you can tell what the favourite is.

You can create folders to store similar types of website. If you are going on holiday, for instance, you can store the airline, travel agent and the hotel website addresses all in the same folder.

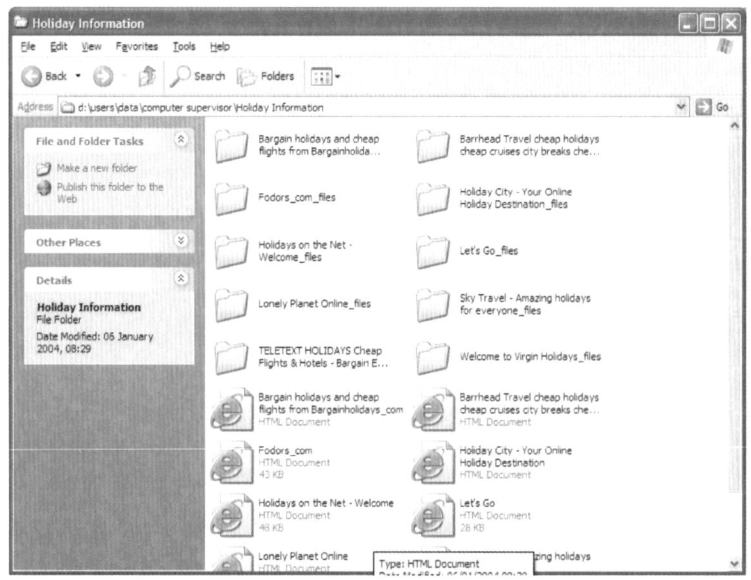

PC MASTER TIP

Keep your Favorites up-to-date. Check that all the links work and that they are in the correct folders. Delete any old or unused sites.

SKILL IN ACTION

Cassie the Cook uses the internet every day for her job and her social life. She has two email addresses from two different providers, one for work and one for family and friends. She also uses websites to order new stock for the kitchen and various websites that have good recipes on them.

Cassie has created a folder to store her two email accounts in. She has other folders to put the recipe sites and the suppliers' sites in.

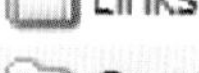

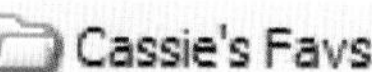

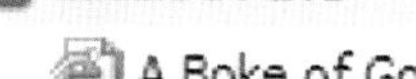

Cassie is moving house so she creates a new folder to store estate agents' websites in.

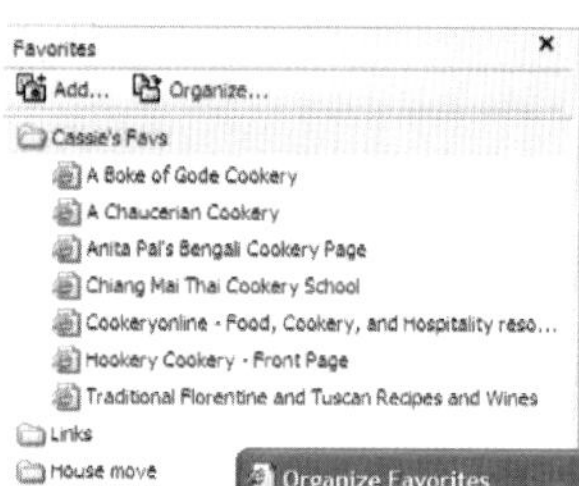

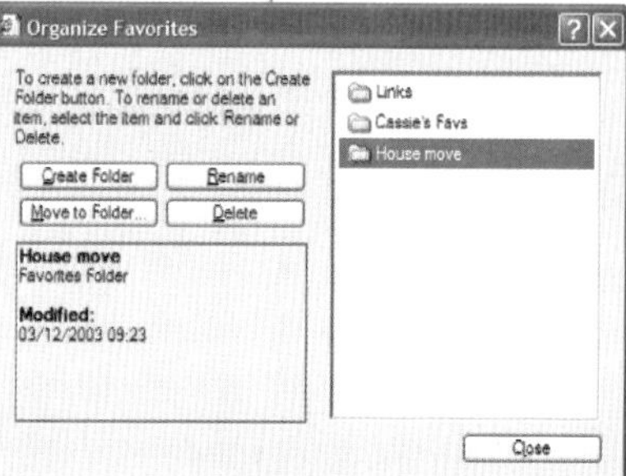

EXERCISE

Save a website in your Favorites.

SKILLS

.: Favorites icon :.

Once you have found a website that you wish to add to your favourites, click on the **Favorites** icon in the toolbar marked with a star.

.: Add and Organize options :.

A new section will appear on the left-hand side of the screen. There are two options at the top of this: **Add** and **Organize**.

.: Favorites window :.

To add a favorite, simply click the **Add** button and a new window will appear. Decide what you are going to call the link and then click **OK**. Your saved favorite will appear in the section on the left-hand side after two or three seconds.

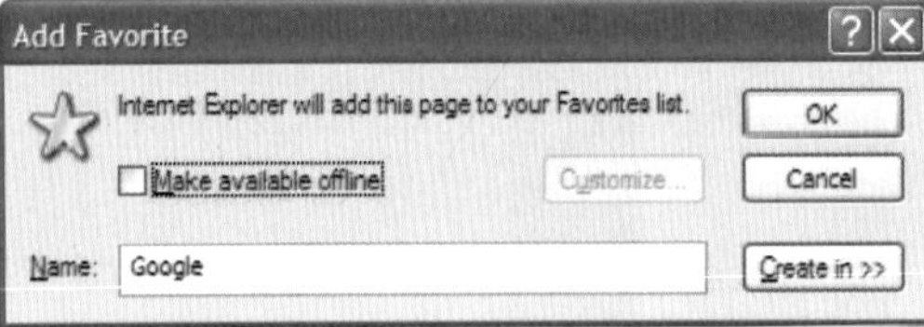

.: Organising favorites :.

You can organise your favorites into folders by selecting the **Organize** button.

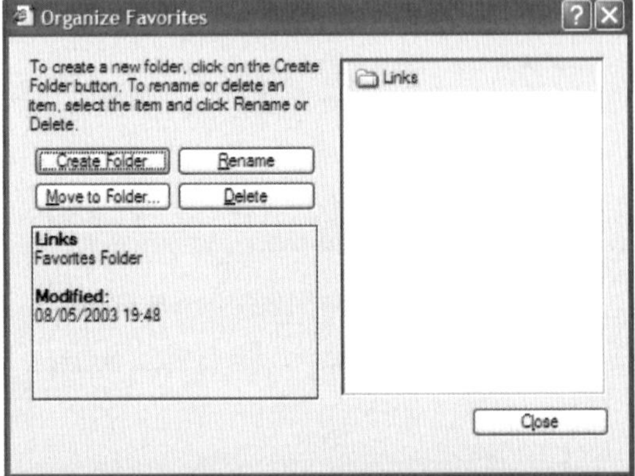

PC MASTER TIP

Your favorites will be kept in alphabetical order. If you want to choose a specific order, rename the sites so that they start with a number.

PROGRESS CHECK EXERCISE

Can you add a favorite website?

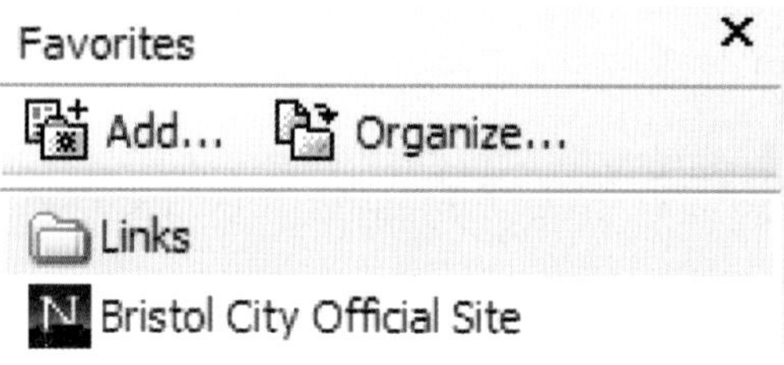

Can you create a folder and drag and drop your favorites into the folder?

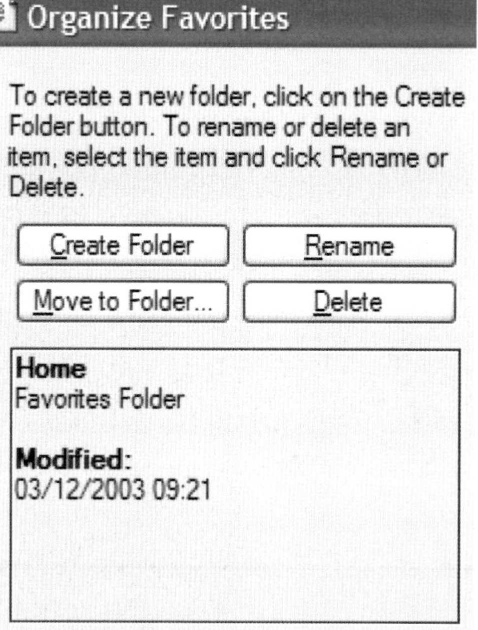

Can you delete a favorite website?

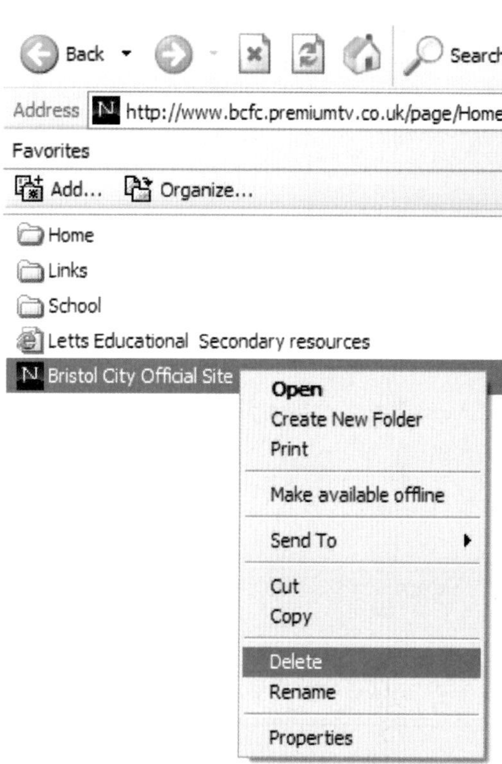

This will only remove your link to the website, not the website itself, so you will be able to find it again.

MASTERCLASS

Can you organise your favorites into similar folders, e.g. email, search engines and travel links?

USING THE WEB TOOLBAR

01001010110100101001011101001010101110101011011100001010111

SKILLS

.: Browser toolbar :.

Whenever you use the internet, you will probably want to view a previously viewed website, find a website that you have just been to or print out some information. The tools at the top of the web browser page will help you do all of these tasks.

There are fourteen icons on the standard Internet Explorer toolbar. Some you will find you use often, others never. You can customize your toolbar by taking off tools you do not use.

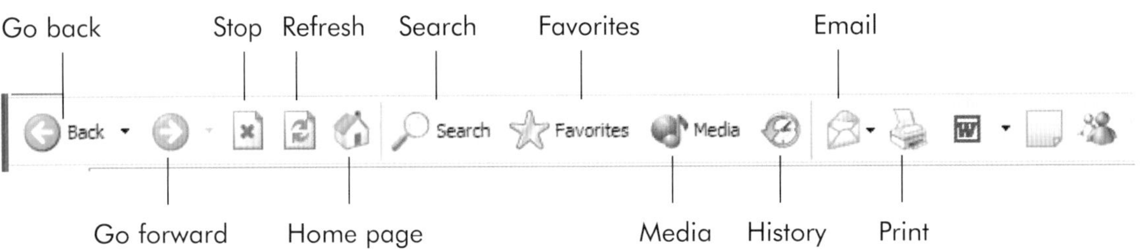

.: Setting up icons :.

Your computer will need to be set up so that some of the icons on the toolbar function correctly. For instance, the email icon will have to be linked to your email account to access it.

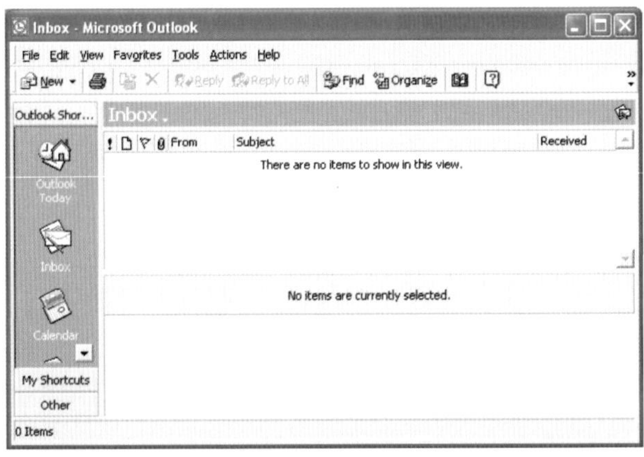

PC MASTER TIP

Once you get used to using all the icons, you will find your work speeds up dramatically.

SKILL IN ACTION

Max the Marketing Executive uses the internet every day for his job. He has hundreds of files stored on his computer. They include music, animations, videos and still images. Max also has a lot of sites saved in Favorites.

When Max uses the internet he uses all the icons on the toolbar because he is constantly flicking from one page to the next and back again.

When he emails someone, he sometimes needs to attach a file. His computer is set up so the email icon logs him on to his email account. If he needs to attach a file, he can search for it using the media window after clicking the media icon.

Media icon 

EXERCISE

Go on to the internet and use each one of the buttons. You do not need to test the print icon as this will print the page automatically.

Untitled - Message (Plain Text)

File Edit View Insert Format Tools Actions Help

Options...

To...

Cc...

SKILLS

.: Navigation icons :.

The first two icons in the web toolbar are navigation tools. They help you to return to previously viewed web pages and then forward again to the current page.

.: Stop icon :.

This will stop the download of a website that you do not want. Some pages contain images that take a long time to download.

.: Refresh icon :.

If you have changed part of a website you are building, or viewing a regularly updated website, click the **Refresh** icon.

.: Home icon :.

Click the **Home** icon and your home page will appear.

.: Search icon :.

This will open a search engine at the side of the page. Type in key words and browse the results. Clicking an option will take the main part of the page to that site.

.: Favorites icon :.

See the previous unit for information about the **Favorites** icon.

.: Media icon :.

The **Media** icon will take you to view your folders: My music, My videos, etc.

.: History icon :.

The **History** icon shows all the websites visited over a period. Every page you visit is logged and the URL is stored in a temporary folder. This list shows all the sites in the order that you have visited them. You cannot delete them from here, and on a network you cannot delete them unless you have administrator rights of access.

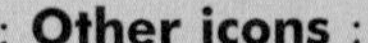

.: Other icons :.

The rest of the icons deal with communication and printing. Computers are set up in different ways so these icons will react differently depending on whether your computer is a stand-alone or linked to a network.

PROGRESS CHECK EXERCISE

Can you select a previously viewed web page from the History window?

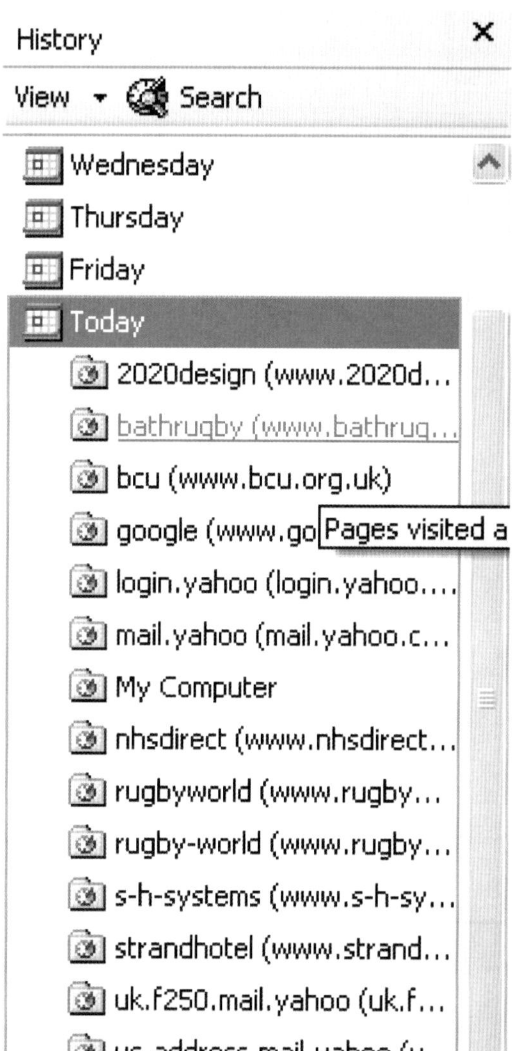

Can you view previously viewed web pages using the Back icon?

Can you return to the Home page?

Can you open your favourites windows?

Can you stop a page loading if it is taking too long?

Can you open the search window?

MASTERCLASS

Can you use the Search tool to find a specific website? Do you think the Search tool is better than using a normal search engine?

SKILLS

.: Email address :.

Email or electronic mail is a method of communicating between two or more people using the internet. To use email you need an email address, just as you do if you want to receive something through the post.

An email address is made up of three parts: the person, the company or mail provider and an ending which generally indicates where the person is emailing from, for example:

pcmaster@lettsed.co.uk

.: Using a mailbox :.

To use email you will need to log on to your mailbox. This requires a password decided by you when you set up your account. You also need the email address of the person you want to email.

In your mailbox, you will be able to store people's email addresses in an address book, check your inbox and compose new emails.

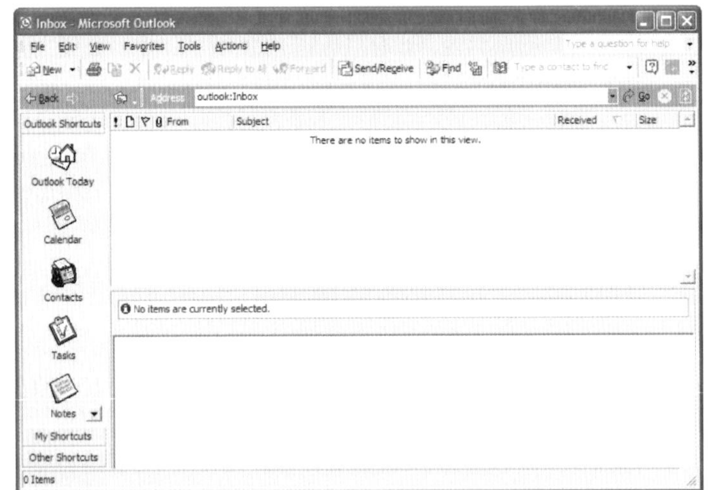

PC MASTER TIP

Unfortunately, people sometimes get a lot of unwanted emails from companies and individuals. This is called junk mail or spam. It is possible to block spam but some can still get into your inbox.

SKILL IN ACTION

Nick the Newspaper Editor has reporters working for him all over the world. They report back to him on events that are taking place in the countries where they work. All the reporters have laptop computers, satellite mobile phones and digital cameras.

This system enables the reporters to email their reports back to Nick in the London office as quickly as possible.

Nick can combine reports from different reporters by inserting them on to the page. As the documents are received electronically, he does not have to retype them, he can just make any alterations he needs.

He can also send his alterations back to the reporters immediately so that they can check that they are happy with them before going to print.

Finally, Nick can then finalise the reports and send them to the printers via email so that they can go into the newspaper.

Existing Yahoo! users

Enter your ID and password to sign in

Yahoo! ID:

Password:

☐ Remember my ID on this computer

Sign In

Mode: Standard | Secure

Sign-in help Forgot your password?

EXERCISE

If you do not have an email address, set one up using one of the free email services that are available online.

SKILLS

.: Using email :.

There are hundreds of different email systems, which are changing all the time. The instructions that follow are fairly general in order to cover as many systems as possible. All systems require the same information to send and receive an email.

.: Compose email window :.

After logging on to your email account using your username and password, press the **Compose** or **New Message** icon. This will open a new window which will have several fields to fill in before you type your message.

.: Composing an email :.

Fill in the address for the person you are sending the mail to. Make sure that the address is correct. It is useful to give the message a title/subject in the **Subject** field.

Type in your message. The message can be as long or as short as you like.

.: Send and read emails :.

Once you have done all this and you are happy with your message, press **Send**.

To read an email, click on the **Inbox** in your email account home page. Click on any messages that are marked 'Unread'.

PC MASTER TIP

Remember that emails are delivered immediately. Check that they are correct before you press Send. You cannot get them back!

PROGRESS CHECK EXERCISE

Can you open your email account?

Can you reply to an email that has been sent to you?

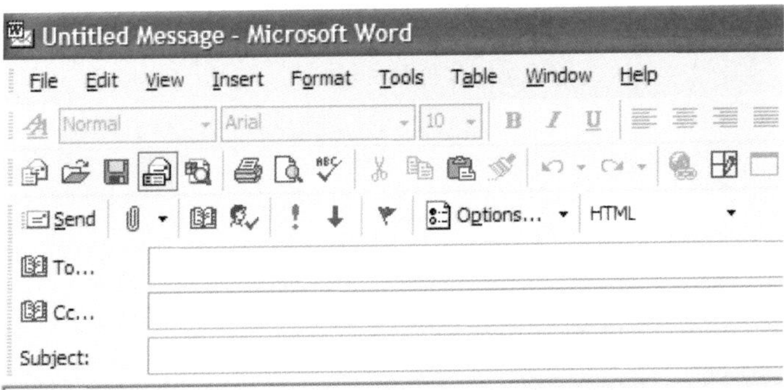

Can you send an email to another person and open a reply when it returns?

Can you send the same message to a lot of people all at the same time?

You can use the carbon copy field or CC on the Compose Message screen.

Can you set up a web based email account?

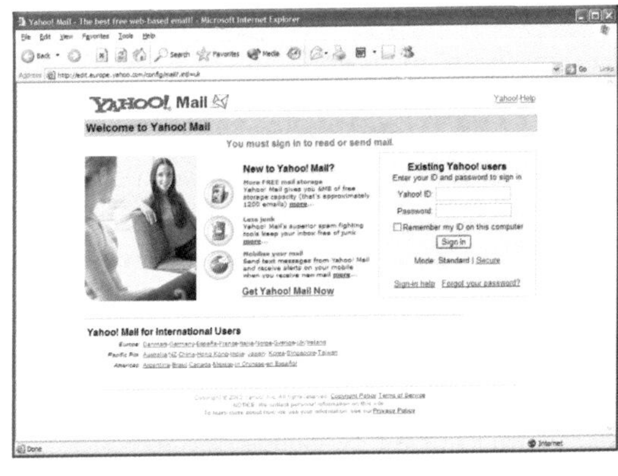

MASTERCLASS

Can you send a copy to lots of people without them knowing it is a copy?

HINT: Try using the blind copy or BCC field on the Compose Message screen.

SKILLS

.: Attachments :.

Sometimes you want to send a file with a message. This is called an **attachment**. Different emailing systems have different methods of attachment but the principle is the same with all of them.

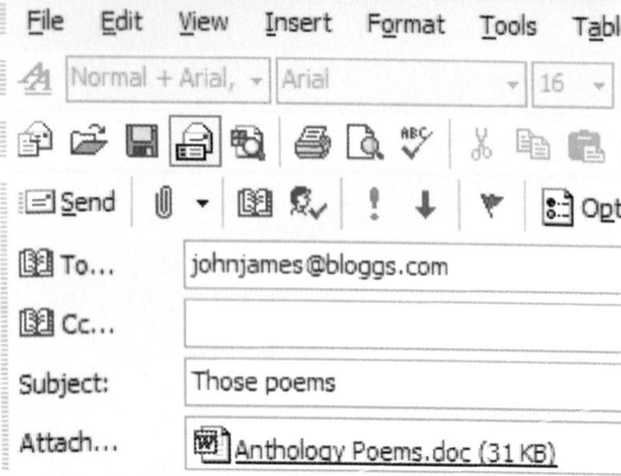

.: Attachments :.

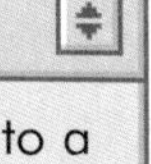

An attachment is a file that is linked to a message. When the message is sent, a copy of the file is sent too. Some mailing systems, especially the free ones, restrict the number or size of the files that you can attach.

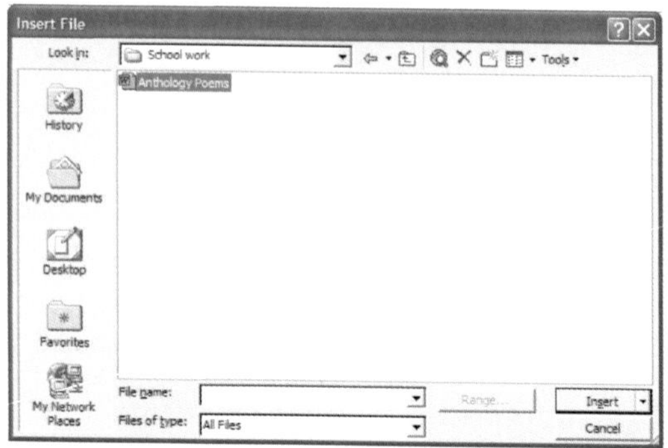

.: Saving attachments :.

When you receive an attachment you can download the file and save it to your computer. However, you must have the correct software to view the file.

PC MASTER TIP

Some files transfer easily. Others require small alterations before they are sent. For example, some images need to be changed into a different file type in order to transfer them more easily.

SKILL IN ACTION

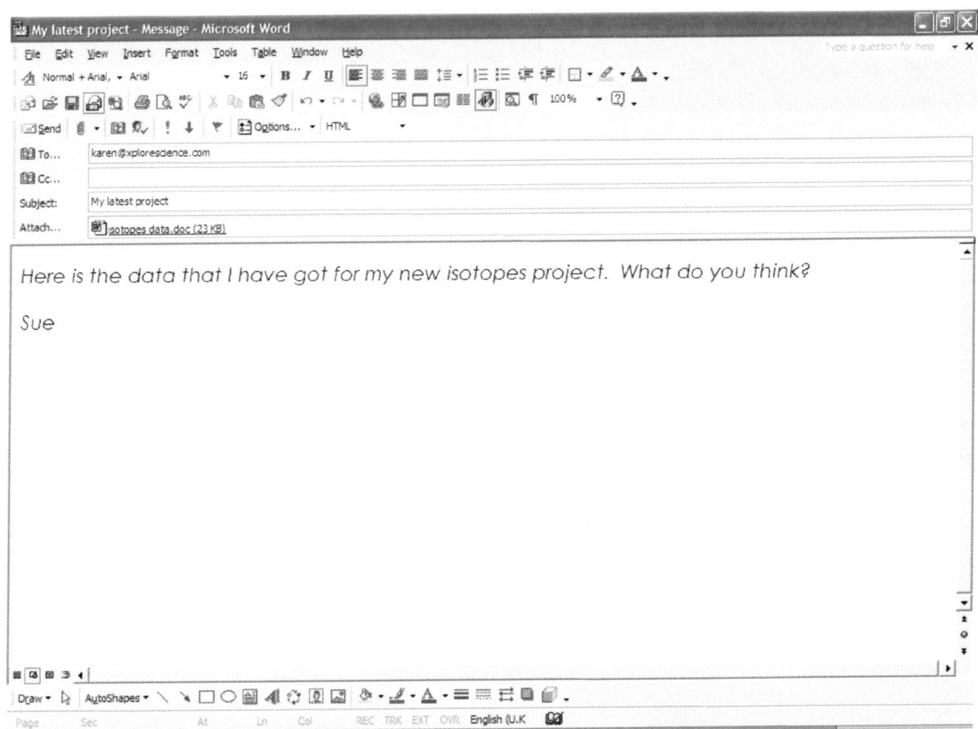

Sue the Scientist uses her computer to send emails every day. She often sends messages to a friend from university, Karen, who lives in America. As Sue's job requires her to collect data during her experiments, she stores the data in different forms on her computer.

Sometimes Sue sends the data she has collected to her friend Karen so that Karen can give Sue her opinion on the results. She attaches the data to the messages she sends.

EXERCISE

Send an email to yourself with an attachment. When you receive it, download it to your computer.

SKILLS

.: Adding an attachment :.

Once you have typed in the email address and the subject, type your message as normal. When you have finished, click the **add attachment** icon, which is close to the message field.

Add attachment icon

.: Add a file :.

Next, press the **Add File** button and browse your documents folders for the file you want to attach. Once you have found it, click **Open**. The file will appear in the field labelled Attached Files.

When you have attached the file or files, click the **Attach File** or **Done** button and the files will be attached to your message. Send the message by pressing **Send**.

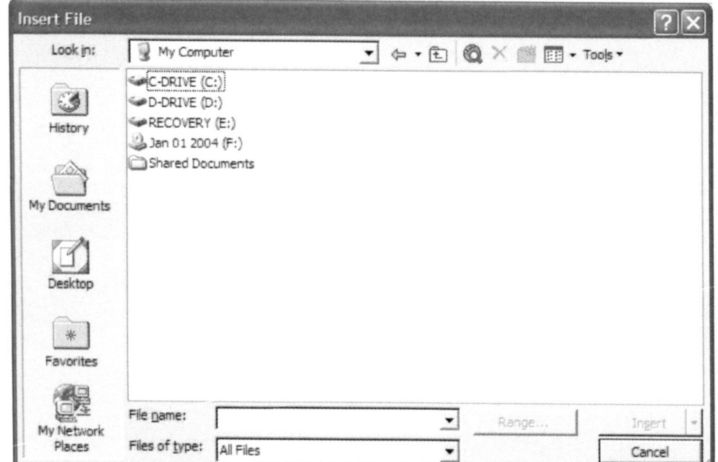

PC MASTER TIP

Some email programs use a paper clip as the add attachment icon.

PROGRESS CHECK EXERCISE

Can you send an email?

Can you attach a file to a message you have written and send it?

Can you attach more than one file to a message?

Can you attach a photo to an email to send to a friend?

Can you see how much memory you are allowed to use when sending attachments? This is sometimes restricted.

Status	From	Subject	Date
	t.joy	☐ attachment	28/11/2003

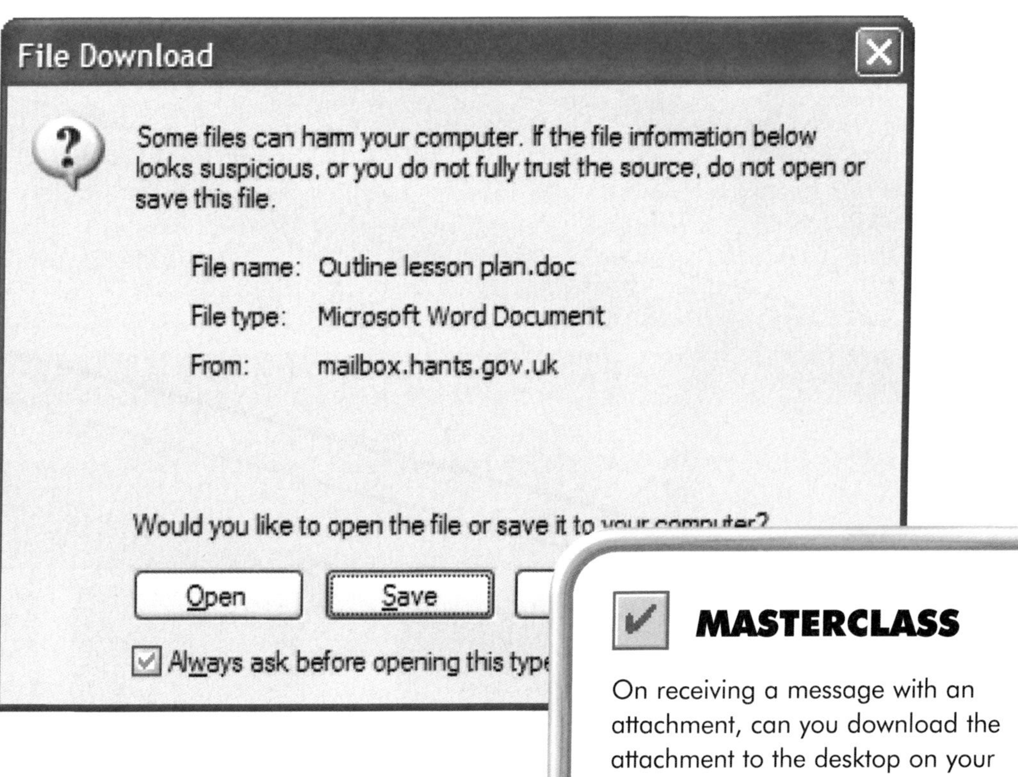

File Download
Some files can harm your computer. If the file information below looks suspicious, or you do not fully trust the source, do not open or save this file.
File name: Outline lesson plan.doc
File type: Microsoft Word Document
From: mailbox.hants.gov.uk
Open
Save
Always ask before opening this type

MASTERCLASS

On receiving a message with an attachment, can you download the attachment to the desktop on your computer?

SKILLS

.: Preparing files for transfer :.

One of the biggest benefits of the internet is the fact that files can be transferred easily and quickly. You can work on a project and send the work to someone else for their comments and receive their feedback the same day. There are various ways to make sure that the file you want to send will transfer as quickly as possible. This is usually done by saving the file in a format that uses as little memory as possible.

.: Picture files :.

The best example of this is picture files. These are often saved as bitmap files, which take up lots of memory and which take a long time to download once the person has received the email. A **jpeg** is a better format in which to send picture files. It is easy to convert pictures from bitmaps to jpegs on most image creation or manipulation software.

.: Compatible software :.

Another problem in transferring files is that the receiver might not have exactly the same software as the sender. There are files which open easily in all applications but there are also files that are software-specific. You need to find out which version of Office the sender is using because if they are using Office 98 and you send them an Office XP file, it will not open. A text file (txt) will always open, no matter what word processor is being used.

Microsoft Word

An error occurred while importing this file. D:\Users\Data\Supervisor\My Pictures\Art Gallery\computer 1.psd

OK

PC MASTER TIP

Before starting your work, decide whether you need to send it to anybody. If you do, think about what format the work needs to be in so that the person you are sending the work to can open it easily.

SKILL IN ACTION

Dave the Designer often has to send his work to clients to show how the work is progressing. He finishes the draft design and sends the image file to everyone who needs to see it. He uses Adobe Photoshop to create his images, but he knows that some of his clients have not got this software.

He wants to send exactly the same file to everyone, so he saves the image as a jpeg file. If he saved it as a Photoshop file, some clients would be able to see exactly what he has done and the file size would be small, but others would not be able to open it. If he sends it as a bitmap file, all his clients could see the file, but it would take ages to send and receive it. To solve this problem, Dave sends the file as a jpeg file to everyone.

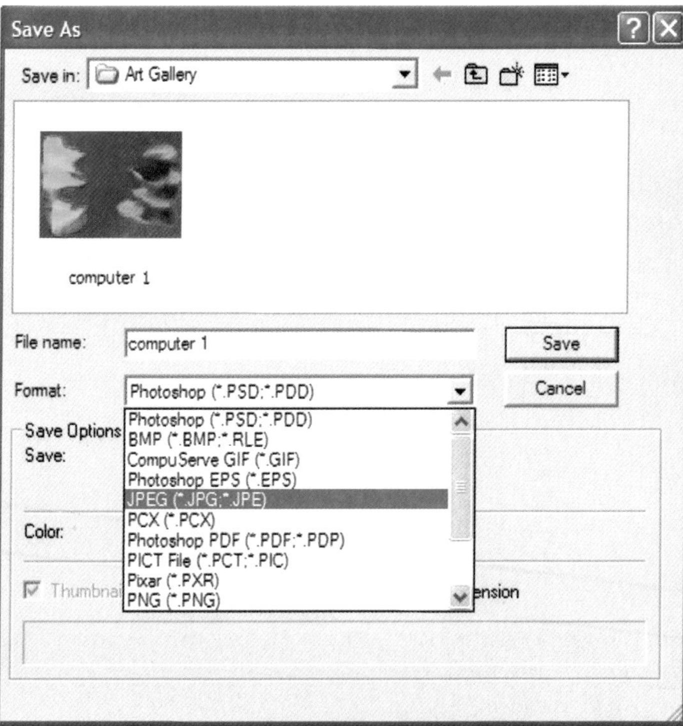

EXERCISE

Can you save an image as a jpeg file?

SKILLS

.: Preparing Word files :.

This is not a difficult skill but you need to understand the different file types. If you have started the document in an application, the application normally saves the file as a default type. This means that unless you specify otherwise, it will save the file in a certain way. Microsoft® Word documents are always saved as doc files, unless you choose to save them as a different type.

If you know that the person you are sending the file to has an older version of Word, you can save the file in the version they have. If you are not sure, you should send the file as a text file (txt) or a rich text format file (rtf). There are many that can be used.

Word Document

Word Document
Web Page
Web Page, Filtered
Web Archive
Document Template
Rich Text Format

.: Preparing Excel files :.

If you are sending a spreadsheet and are not sure of the version of Excel the other person has, or are not sure that the receiver even has Excel, it is a good idea to send the file in a different form.

Excel files are normally saved as xls files, but if you save them as comma separated variable files (csv), they should open on most spreadsheet applications.

Microsoft Excel Workbook

Microsoft Excel Workbook
Web Page
Web Archive
XML Spreadsheet
Template
Text (Tab delimited)

.: Preparing image files :.

There are lots of ways to send images. Application-specific software is the least likely to transfer well but there are many files that will open on most image software. The most common are bitmaps (bmp), jpegs (jpg) or gifs (gif).

PC MASTER TIP

Be careful when changing the file type because sometimes the text loses its formatting. If this happens, you will need to change the font, size and colour again once it has been received.

PROGRESS CHECK EXERCISE

Can you save a Word file as a text file?

Can you change the file type of an image to a jpeg?

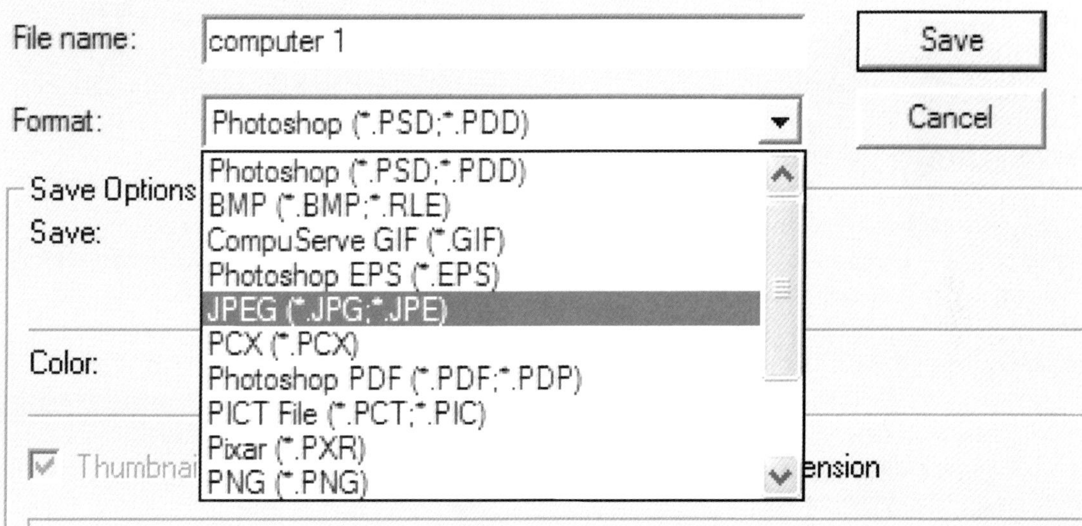

Yellow year
Microsoft Excel Worksheet
43 KB

Yellow Year 2003
Microsoft Excel Comma Separ...
7 KB

Yellow Year 2003
Microsoft Excel Worksheet
54 KB

Yellow Year 20032
Microsoft Excel Comma Separ...
4 KB

Can you save a spreadsheet as a csv file?

Can you open it again in Excel?

MASTERCLASS

Can you save an Excel spreadsheet as a text file and then convert it back into a spreadsheet?

SKILLS

.: Virus checking :.

There are lots of things that you might want to download from the internet. You might receive attachments to an email that you want to download. You might find files to help you do your work, or you might want to download some shareware.

All of this is easy to do, but you might also accidentally download a virus. This is a small computer program that can reproduce itself and then copy itself from one computer to another. A virus can be capable of destroying all the data on a computer. If you are opening an attachment to an email, your email provider normally supplies a virus check service for you.

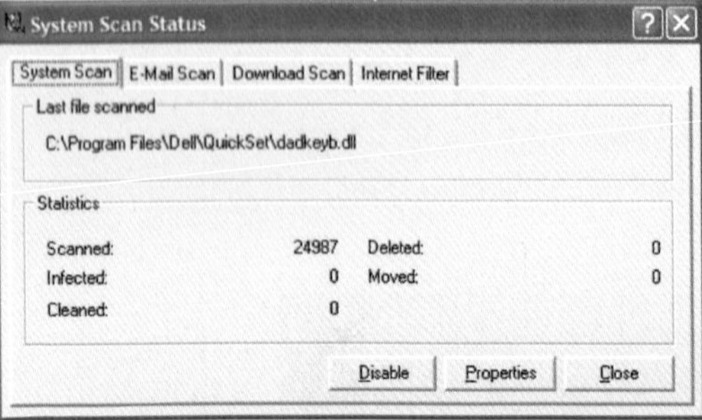

.: Downloading a file :.

You should have your own virus checker running to check files. If you want to download a program or file from the internet, it is usually made very clear how to start the process and you simply follow instructions on the screen.

To download files from the internet, you can either click on the link to download the file or you can right click on the link and select **Save Target As.** This will save the file to your computer.

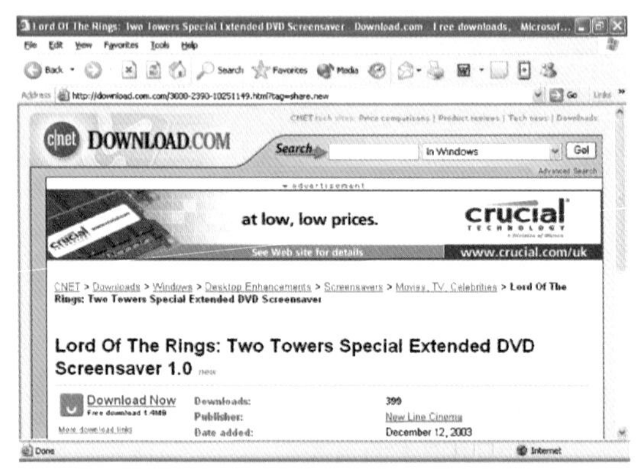

PC MASTER TIP

Shareware is not the same as freeware. Freeware is a completely free program. Shareware might just be a demonstration version of the program, or it might be a limited time trial version to try before buying the full version.

SKILL IN ACTION

Tammy the Teacher uses www.teachit.co.uk to download worksheets for lessons. This website is designed for English teachers and has lots of resources linked to the National Curriculum. It is a commercial site and they charge for full access to the site, but Tammy just uses the resources available to her.

Tammy is doing some work on Animal Farm with Year 9 pupils. As she is going to be on a course next week she looks for a worksheet to leave the class with while she is away. She finds a good worksheet on this website and wants to download it.

Tammy follows the on-screen instructions and saves the file in her Year 9 folder.

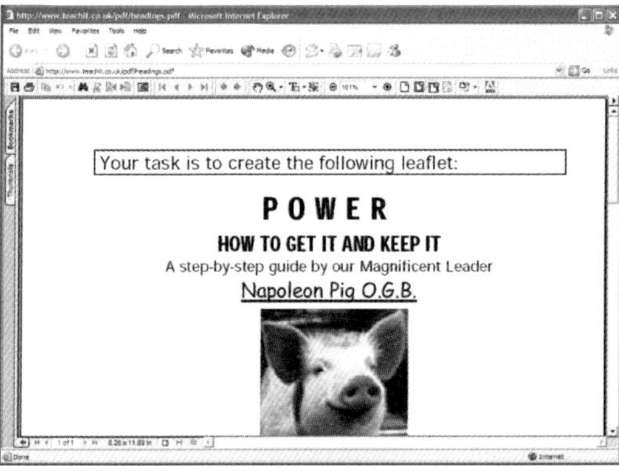

EXERCISE

Can you find a worksheet on your favourite book and save it on your computer? There are lots of websites that can help you.

SKILLS

.: Email attachments :.

If you have an email attachment to download, it usually appears as a link under the subject box on the email.

.: Download the attachments :.

Click on the link to begin the download process. The computer will ask you if you want to save the file to disk or just open it. If you choose to open it, you can still save it later.

File Download

Some files can harm your computer. If the file information below looks suspicious, or you do not fully trust the source, do not open or save this file.

File name: Outline lesson plan.doc
File type: Microsoft Word Document
From: mailbox.hants.gov.uk

Would you like to open the file or save it to your computer?

Open | Save | Cancel | More Info

☑ Always ask before opening this type of file

.: Download software :.

If you want to download a shareware program, as long as you are using a good shareware website, you will be given exact instructions to follow. There is normally a **Download Here** button to click on.

.: Download options :.

To download a file, either click on the link to download the file or right click on the link and select **Save Target As** from the following menu:

Open
Open in New Window
Save Target As...
Print Target
Cut
Copy
Copy Shortcut
Paste
Add to Favorites...
Properties

PC MASTER TIP

There are sometimes several choices of file to download. Make sure that you are downloading the version that will work on your computer.

PROGRESS CHECK EXERCISE

Can you attach a file to an email and send it to yourself? Now download the attachment and save it in a new folder in your My Documents folder.

Can you find a demonstration version of a computer game or software? Download it on to your computer and check that it works. Uninstall it using the Add/Remove Programs icon in the control panel.

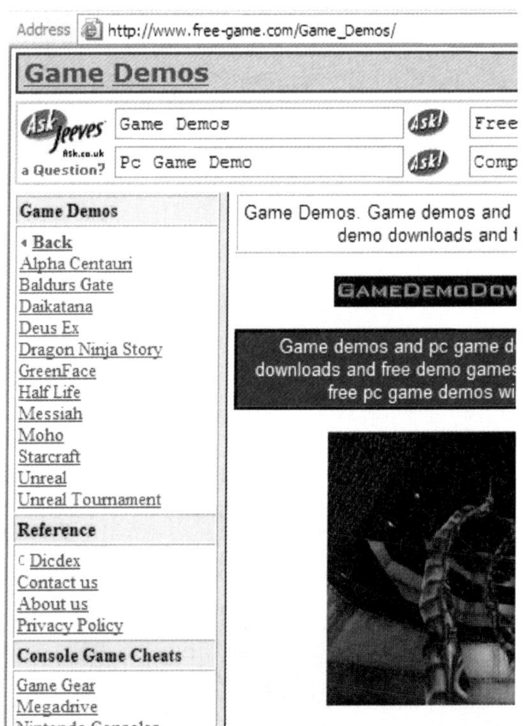

Can you download an mp3 file from a free mp3 website?

Can you download mp3 player software to play the file? This will have to be a demonstration version as they all charge a small fee for the full program. Below is an example of the software that you might find.

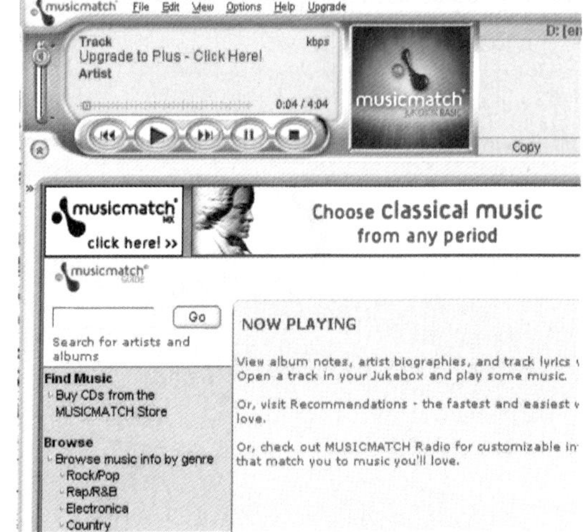

MASTERCLASS

Can you find a website that contains drivers for the computer equipment that you have got? This will be really useful if your scanner, printer, or camera stops working on your computer. Downloading new drivers could be the solution to the problem.

SKILLS

.: Building a website :.

If you want to build a website but do not have any suitable software, you can create it using Notepad or WordPad. These programs come free with most computers and are very simple to use.

Notepad

WordPad

.: Using HTML :.

There is another advantage to using these programs over web authoring software and that is that they generally use a lot less memory. However, you need to know how to use the language. This is called **HTML**, which stands for HyperText Markup Language. The process of writing HTML is actually fairly simple. If you are putting in a command and the writing is not actually going to appear on the web page, it needs to be between two arrows <like this>. This is called a **tag**. If you want the writing to appear, you need to make sure that it is not between the arrows. If you have changed something, you must stop the change at the end of the line so the computer knows what to do. There are certain commands that you need to know about before you start.

- At the start of a page, you need to type <HTML>. At the end of the page, you type </HTML>.
- At the start of a heading, type <HEAD> and at the end </HEAD>. At the start of a title, type <TITLE> and at the end, type </TITLE>.

The rest of the text needs to go between <BODY> and </BODY>. This is how you start a web page.

PC MASTER TIP

If you really want to learn HTML, have a look on the internet for more information. There are so many tags that you can use, you need a reference guide to help you.

SKILL IN ACTION

Ahmed the Artist has a website for selling his paintings but he does not have Microsoft® FrontPage or any other web authoring software. He keeps the website up-to-date by adapting it in Notepad. He has been learning HTML for a while now and has the confidence to write the website in that program.

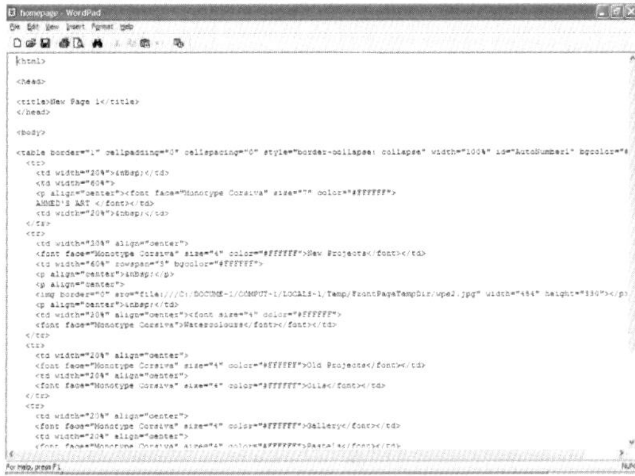

Once Ahmed has finished writing the page, he saves it as an HTML file.

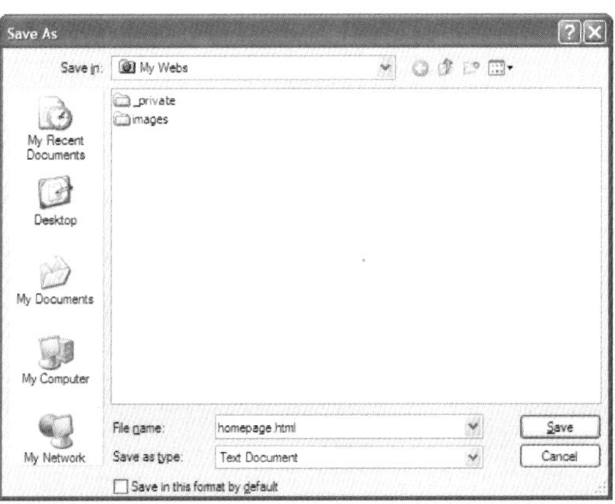

He double clicks on the file to open it. It automatically opens in Internet Explorer.

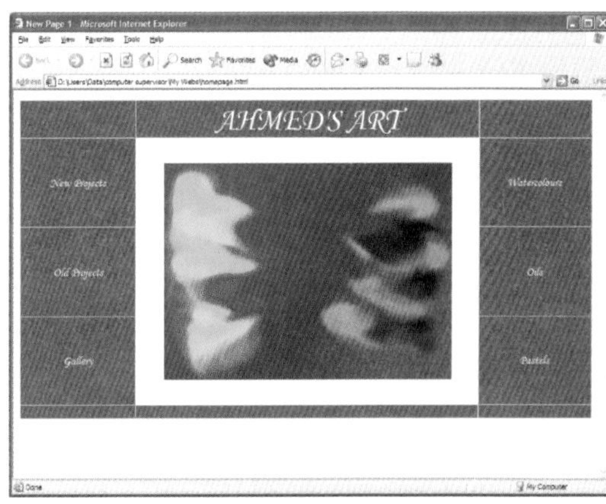

EXERCISE

Can you make a basic web page with a title?

SKILLS

.: How to write HTML :.

The easiest way to learn HTML is to become familiar with all the most useful tags and to understand what they do. Here are some of the common ones:

 — This inserts a line break.

Start tags <B>, <I>, <U>
End tags </B>, </I>, </U> — These tags make the font bold, italic or underlined.

<FONT SIZE=12>text in size 12 font goes here</FONT. — This makes the writing the font size that you want it.

<BODY BGCOLOUR=#000000> — This makes the background colour black (#FFFFFF is white).

<A HREF="www.letts-education.co.uk"> click here for link to Letts website</A> — This will create a link to www.letts-education.co.uk and will write "Click here for link to Letts website" as the link.

<IMG SRC="c:\my documents\logo.jpg"> — This will insert an image called logo at this point. You will need to include the details of where the image is saved. In this case, it is on the C:/ drive in a folder called **My Documents**.

.: Save your file :.

To save the file, save it as a web page by adding **.html** to the end of the file name and double click to open it in your browser.

PC MASTER TIP

In order to put your website on the internet, you will need to contact your Internet Service Provider and pay them for the use of their web server.

PROGRESS CHECK EXERCISE

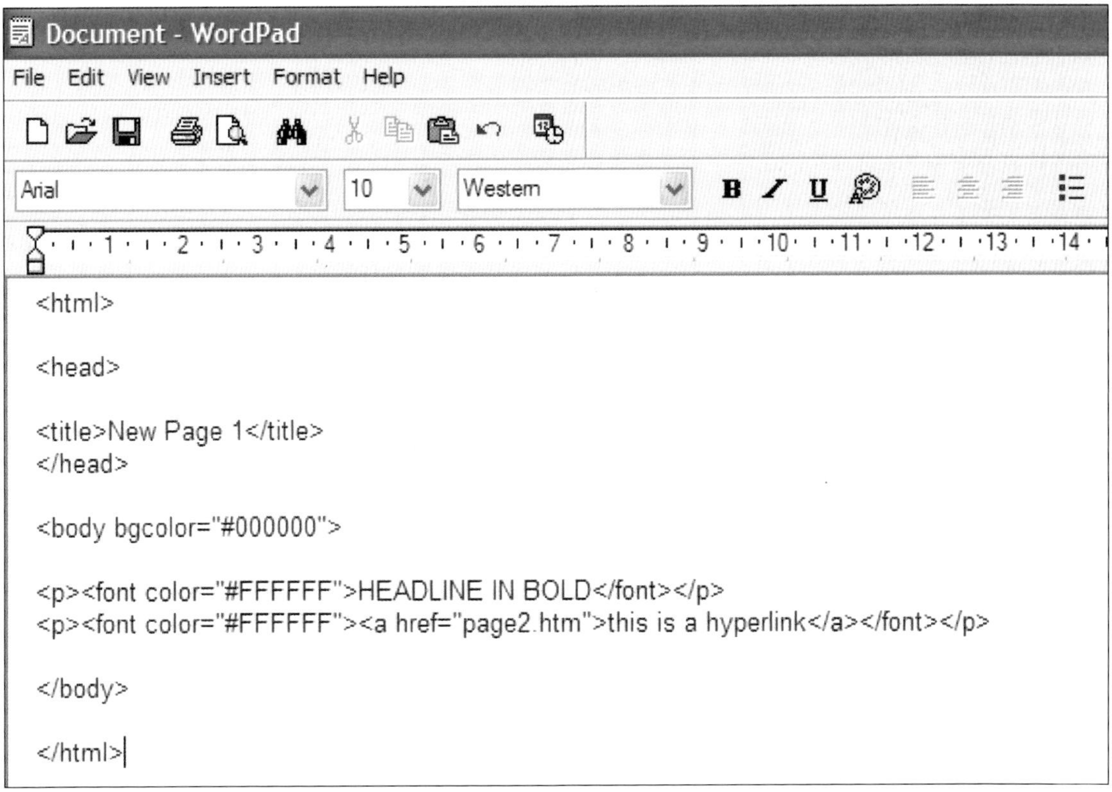

Document - WordPad

File Edit View Insert Format Help

```
<html>

<head>

<title>New Page 1</title>
</head>

<body bgcolor="#000000">

<p><font color="#FFFFFF">HEADLINE IN BOLD</font></p>
<p><font color="#FFFFFF"><a href="page2.htm">this is a hyperlink</a></font></p>

</body>

</html>
```

Type the information above in Notepad or WordPad. Can you work out what the web page will look like?

Try to alter the background so that the colour is #FF0000. What colour is it?

Can you write a simple HTML page that contains a background and a title? Look at the source information on the previous tasks if you get stuck.

MASTERCLASS

Try to create a web page with a green background and blue writing. It should contain a hyperlink to the Letts website and one other website of your choice.

VIEW SOURCE

SKILLS

.: View source :.

This is a very useful thing to know about if you are thinking of learning HTML to write websites. All websites can be seen in HTML view by using this function, but the more complicated the site, the more difficult it is to see what has been done.

ddchomea[1] - Notepad

File Edit Format View Help

```
<html>
<head>
<title>WinZip&reg; - Download Evaluation Page</title>
</head>
<body bgcolor="#000000"  text="#FFFFFF" vlink="#AADBFF" LINK="#D9B800">
<CENTER>
<TABLE CELLSPACING=0 CELLPADDING=0 border=0 WIDTH=600 align=center>
<!--  -->
<!-- header -->
<TR align=left><TD align=left colspan=5 width=600 height=11><IMG SRC="http://image.winzip.co
<!-- bluedots and glow -->
<TR ALIGN="left">
<TD ALIGN="left" VALIGN="TOP" WIDTH=36 height=110><IMG SRC="http://image.winzip.com/bludots.
<!--  -->
<TD ALIGN="center" VALIGN="bottom" WIDTH=224 HEIGHT=110><img src="http://image.winzip.com/do
<!--  -->
<TD ALIGN="LEFT" VALIGN="TOP" WIDTH=125 HEIGHT=110><IMG SRC="http://image.winzip.com/dotb_.g
<TD ALIGN="center" VALIGN="top" WIDTH=69 HEIGHT=110>
<IMG SRC="http://image.winzip.com/dotb_.gif" WIDTH=69 HEIGHT=20 BORDER=0 alt=""><BR>
<A HREF="order.cgi?wza"><IMG SRC="http://image.winzip.com/hotcfin.gif" WIDTH=69 HEIGHT=54 BO
<TD ALIGN="LEFT" VALIGN="bottom" WIDTH=148 HEIGHT=110><IMG SRC="http://image.winzip.com/dotb
</TR>
</TABLE>

<!-- ______________________________ -->

<TABLE CELLSPACING=0 CELLPADDING=0 border=0 WIDTH=600 align=center>
<TR>
<TD ALIGN="center" VALIGN="TOP" width=300>
<FONT face="Arial, Verdana, Helvetica, sans-serif">

<BR>

worldwide download sites available through
```

ddchomea[1] - Notepad

File Edit Format View Help

```
<html>
<head>
<title>WinZip&reg; - Down
</head>
<body bgcolor="#000000"
<CENTER>
<TABLE CELLSPACING=0 CELL
```

.: View source :.

One of the best ways to learn how to write HTML for a specific item on your web page is to find a similar item on somebody else's website and look at how they did it. The source on the left shows the HTML that was used to colour a background. If you do not know the colour code for the colour you want, find a site with a similar colour and copy the code from there.

PC MASTER TIP

You can copy the source information into a word processing document. Delete any code that you do not need. That way the area that you want to use will be clearer to see.

SKILL IN ACTION

Vicrum the Vet decided to learn HTML in order to build a website about the research he is doing. He learnt the basics but wanted to know how to add a hyperlink to his web page. He found a site with a hyperlink,

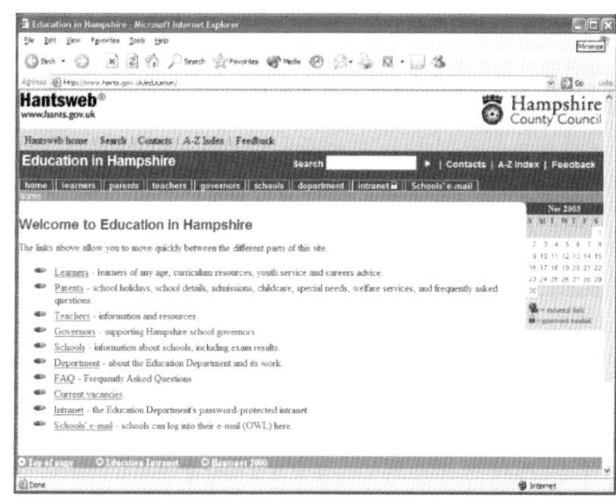

and looked at the source to see how it was done.

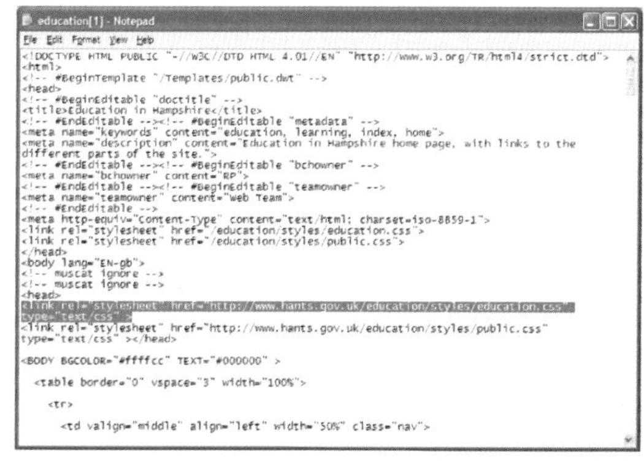

education[1] - Notepad

```
<!DOCTYPE HTML PUBLIC "-//W3C//DTD HTML 4.01//EN" "http://www.w3.org/TR/html4/strict.dtd">
<html>
<!-- #BeginTemplate "/Templates/public.dwt" -->
<head>
<!-- #BeginEditable "doctitle" -->
<title>Education in Hampshire</title>
<!-- #EndEditable --><!-- #BeginEditable "metadata" -->
<meta name="keywords" content="education, learning, index, home">
<meta name="description" content="Education in Hampshire home page, with links to the
different parts of the site.">
<!-- #EndEditable --><!-- #BeginEditable "bchowner" -->
<meta name="bchowner" content="RP">
<!-- #EndEditable --><!-- #BeginEditable "teamowner" -->
<meta name="teamowner" content="Web Team">
<!-- #EndEditable -->
<meta http-equiv="Content-Type" content="text/html; charset=iso-8859-1">
<link rel="stylesheet" href="/education/styles/education.css">
<link rel="stylesheet" href="/education/styles/public.css">
</head>
<body lang="EN-gb">
<!-- muscat ignore -->
<!-- muscat ignore -->
<head>
<link rel="stylesheet" href="http://www.hants.gov.uk/education/styles/education.css"
type="text/css" >
<link rel="stylesheet" href="http://www.hants.gov.uk/education/styles/public.css"
type="text/css" ></head>

<BODY BGCOLOR="#ffffcc" TEXT="#000000" >

  <table border="0" vspace="3" width="100%">

    <tr>

      <td valign="middle" align="left" width="50%" class="nav">
```

Vicrum can now use the code that he has found to add a hyperlink to his own website.

```
<a href="file:///D:/Users/Data/My%20Webs/cats.html">
link to information about cats</a></p>
```

When he has done this, he can view his web page in his browser and check the hyperlink.

EXERCISE

Can you look at the source of a web page and see how the page has been linked to another one?

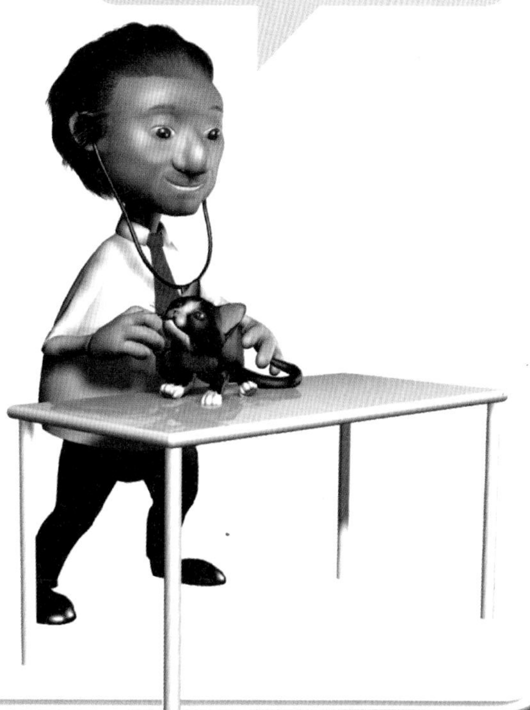

SKILLS

.: Viewing source text :.

To view the source text for a web page you need firstly to find the web page on the internet. Once the page has loaded, select **View** on the main menu bar and then **Source** on the drop down menu.

.: Viewing source text :.

This should automatically open Notepad and the HTML language will appear. The text might not be as long as you would expect for the page. This is because the Notepad file has not been set to word wrap so you cannot see all the text across the page at the same time. To set word wrap, click on **Format** on the main menu bar and then select **Word Wrap**.

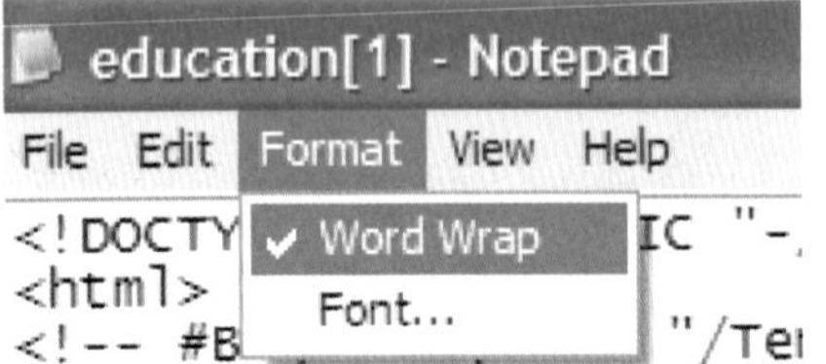

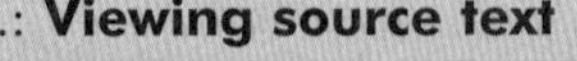

.: Viewing source text :.

Notepad has now made the page on the screen the same width as the page in the document, so the file appears longer (but you can see the whole width).

education[1] - Notepad

File Edit Format View Help

```
<!DOCTYPE HTML PUBLIC "-//W3C//DTD HTML 4.01//EN" "http://www.w3.org/TR/html4/strict.dtd">
<html>
<!-- #BeginTemplate "/Templates/public.dwt" -->
<head>
<!-- #BeginEditable "doctitle" -->
<title>Education in Hampshire</title>
<!-- #EndEditable --><!-- #BeginEditable "metadata" -->
<meta name="keywords" content="education, learning, index, home">
<meta name="description" content="Education in Hampshire home page, with links to the
different parts of the site.">
<!-- #EndEditable --><!-- #BeginEditable "bchowner" -->
<meta name="bchowner" content="RP">
<!-- #EndEditable --><!-- #BeginEditable "teamowner" -->
<meta name="teamowner" content="Web Team">
<!-- #EndEditable -->
<meta http-equiv="Content-Type" content="text/html; charset=iso-8859-1">
<link rel="stylesheet" href="/education/styles/education.css">
<link rel="stylesheet" href="/education/styles/public.css">
</head>
<body lang="EN-gb">
<!-- muscat ignore -->
<!-- muscat ignore -->
<head>
<link rel="stylesheet" href="http://www.hants.gov.uk/education/styles/education.css"
type="text/css" >
<link rel="stylesheet" href="http://www.hants.gov.uk/education/styles/public.css"
type="text/css" ></head>

<BODY BGCOLOR="#ffffcc" TEXT="#000000" >

  <table border="0" vspace="3" width="100%">

    <tr>

      <td valign="middle" align="left" width="50%" class="nav">
```

.: Viewing source text :.

You can copy the text into Word, WordPad or just adapt it. If you save it as an HTML file, you can double click to open it. It should open in your web browser as a web page.

PC MASTER TIP

If you are viewing a page that has frames (a border down the edge of the site), make sure that you are viewing the source you want to see. If you do not do this, you might waste time looking for something that is not in the frame (border) and not in the main section of the site.

PROGRESS CHECK EXERCISE

www.lettsed.co[1] - Notepad

File Edit Format View Help

```
<html>
<head>

<title>Letts Educational : Letts Educational : Student - Key Stage 1</title>
<link rel="stylesheet" href="/home/templates/stylesheet.css" type="text/css">
<script language="javascript">

function siteMap(location) {
    window.open("/showmap.jsp?map=/home/fullmap&location="+location, "glsitemap", "width
}

// -->

</script>
<script language="JavaScript">
<!--
function MM_swapImgRestore() { //v3.0
  var i,x,a=document.MM_sr; for(i=0;a&&i<a.length&&(x=a[i])&&x.oSrc;i++) x.src=x.oSrc;
}

function MM_preloadImages() { //v3.0
  var d=document; if(d.images){ if(!d.MM_p) d.MM_p=new Array();
    var i,j=d.MM_p.length,a=MM_preloadImages.arguments; for(i=0; i<a.length; i++)
    if (a[i].indexOf("#")!=0){ d.MM_p[j]=new Image; d.MM_p[j++].src=a[i];}}
```

Can you view the HTML that has been used to make the ITV website (www.itv.com)?

Can you change the text in a Notepad file so that all the words fit across the screen?

Can you find out how to change the font size on your website by looking at a website with bigger or smaller writing?

Can you find out how to change the colour of the font in HTML by looking at some coloured writing on a website?

MASTERCLASS

Can you see how to make hyperlinks on a web page? Try to make some on a website of your own by copying and pasting the information, then adapting it.

SKILLS

.: Temporary files :.

When you use the internet, each web page that you look at is stored or cached in a special temporary folder inside the Windows folder. These files are stored there because it is highly likely that you will want to use them again in the future. If they have already been downloaded once, it is time-consuming to download them again. Keeping them in a temporary file is more efficient.

Temporary Internet files

Pages you view on the Internet are stored in a special folder for quick viewing later.

Delete Cookies... Delete Files... Settings...

.: Temporary files :.

The size of the folder is limited. If too many files are stored, this can affect the performance of your computer.

PC MASTER TIP

If you do not want people to see what sites you have been looking at, you can clear the history in the Internet Properties window. This will also free up a little space on the hard drive.

SKILL IN ACTION

Sophie the Student uses the internet every day so her computer stores lots of temporary files. She has set the computer to keep the temporary files for eight days.

This means she can revisit a site for a week and not have to download the whole page.

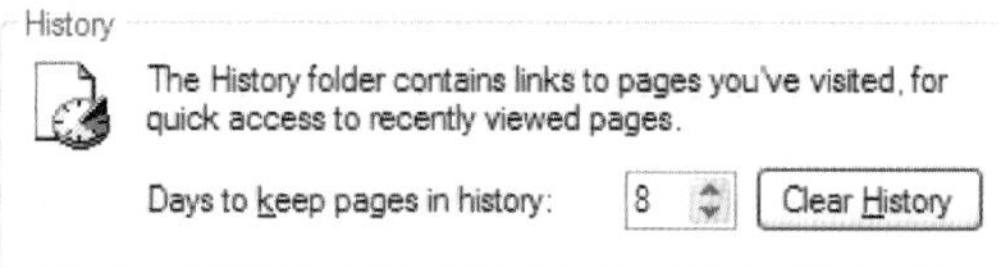

Sophie has also set the amount of space allowed for temporary internet files at 30000 MB, which gives her plenty of space to store them.

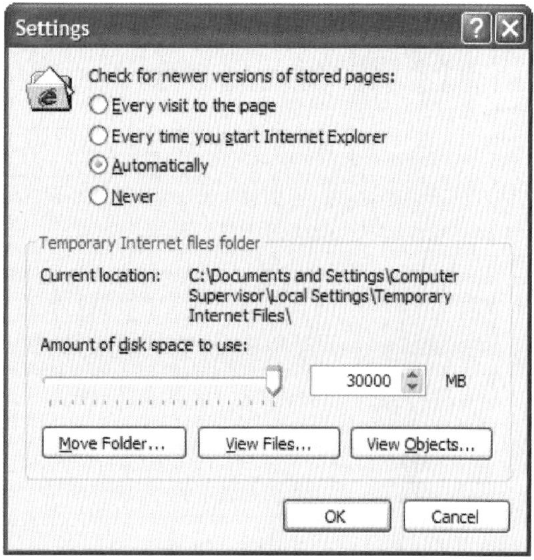

Occasionally Sophie shares her computer with her flat mate. Sophie usually deletes all the temporary internet files and the history so that her work cannot be copied by anyone else.

EXERCISE

Clear the history and temporary internet files from your computer. Note that you will not be able to do this if you are working on a network.

SKILLS

.: Disk Cleanup :.

Click on **Start**, **All Programs**, **Accessories**, **System Tools** and select **Disk Cleanup**. This enables you to delete a number of things, one of which is the temporary internet files.

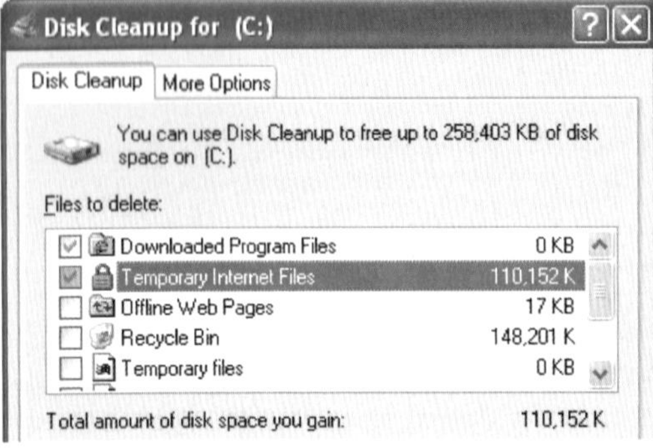

.: Internet options :.

The other method is to click on **Start**, **Control Panel**, **Network and Internet Connections**, and finally on **Internet Options**. Here you can set your home page, edit the settings for the internet temporary files and the settings for the history.

.: Deleting files :.

To delete all the temporary internet files, select the **Delete Files** button in the window. Check the **Delete all offline content**, then click **OK**. The task may take a few seconds because there may be thousands of files to delete.

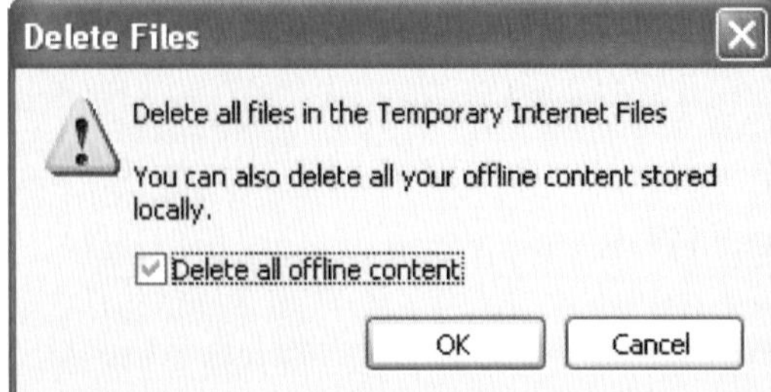

.: Deleting files :.

This will free up some space on your computer but the files will be permanently deleted. They are not sent to the Recycle Bin. As soon as you start using the internet again, more temporary internet files will be created.

PC MASTER TIP

You can change how much space is allocated for saving temporary internet files in the **Internet Options** menu. This could help the performance of your computer.

PROGRESS CHECK EXERCISE

Can you clear all the temporary files using Disk Cleanup?

Can you clear the temporary files using the Internet Options window?

Can you set the settings for the amount of disk space that will allow temporary internet files?

Use the Internet Options window.

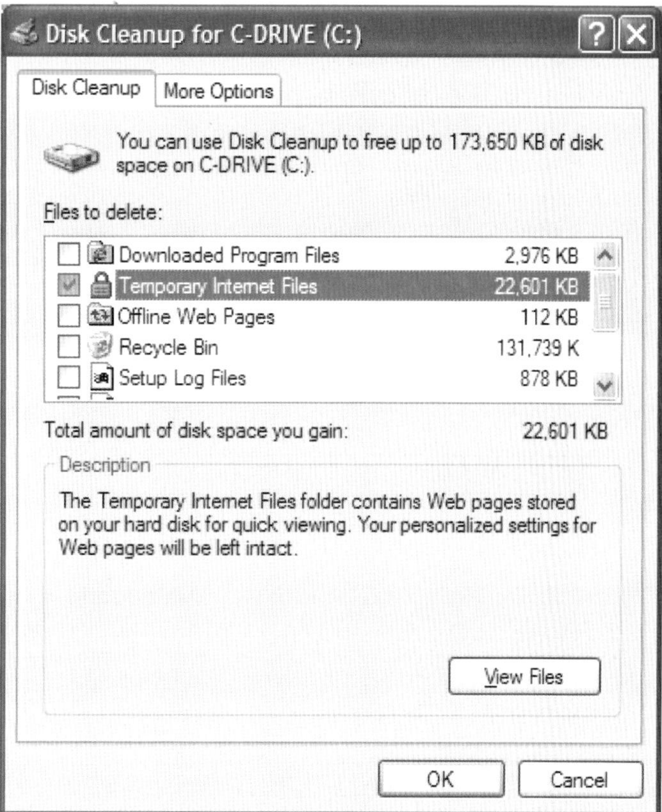

MASTERCLASS

Can you set a routine for doing a health check on your computer once a month?

HINT: Clear unwanted files and use the Disk Defragmenter to organise your files on the hard disk.

SKILLS

.: Advanced searching :.

Searching the internet for information can be a huge task. Sometimes you just cannot find what you need, other times you find so many things that you are not sure what is most useful. There are ways to narrow your search so that you find the most suitable sites. The first and most simple of these is to search only for files from the UK. There is normally an option to do this.

Google Search | I'm Feeling Lucky

Search: ○ the web ◉ pages from the UK

.: Boolean operators :.

You can use Boolean operators to adapt your search. These are words or symbols that can be typed into a search line but will not be searched for themselves. Examples of these are AND, OR, NOT and NEAR. You can also use + and – to narrow down a search.

.: Order searching :.

Another good way of narrowing down a search is to specify the order of the words. If you type 'top ten singles chart', the search engine will search for the words 'top', 'ten', 'singles' and 'chart' in any order or in any combination. If you put the phrase in speech marks, it will treat the phrase as one word. So if you type – "Top ten singles chart", the search engine will only search for these four words where they appear in this order.

Depending on the search engine that you are using, there are different advanced search options that you can use.

PC MASTER TIP

Remember, if you are too specific you might not find any sites at all. Do not be afraid to widen your search.

SKILL IN ACTION

Sophie the Student uses advanced searches when she is researching information for her projects. She often needs to find specific information quickly and she knows that if she is too general in her search, she will find thousands of sites so it will be hard to pinpoint the one that she wants.

She is doing a project on glaciers and she wants to find more information about glaciers in Europe.

Her first search found about 767,000 hits. This means that to find a good site, she would have to look through all these sites. She did an advanced search and this found 236 hits.

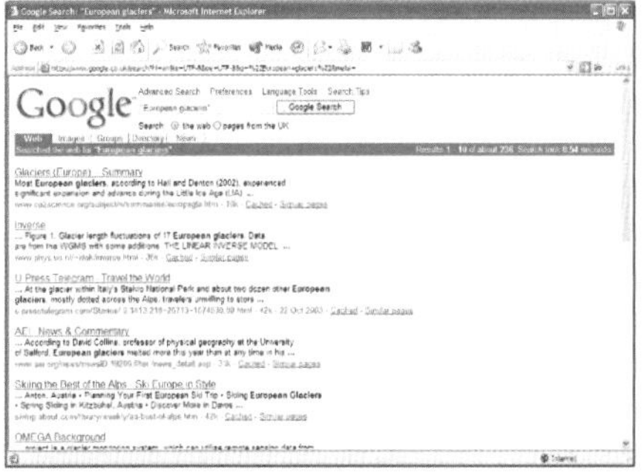

Now Sophie has a much better chance of finding a suitable site. She wants to find more information about Mont Blanc in particular, so she adds this to her search.

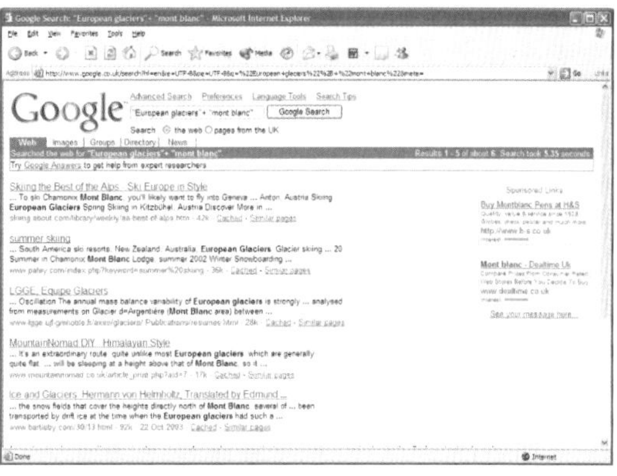

EXERCISE

Can you find some information about Mont Blanc from the internet using an advanced search to find the most relevant websites?

SKILLS

.: Advanced search :.

If you are not sure how the Boolean operators work, you can always use the advanced search options on your search engine to adapt your search.

On www.google.co.uk the **Advanced Search** link brings up the menu on the right:

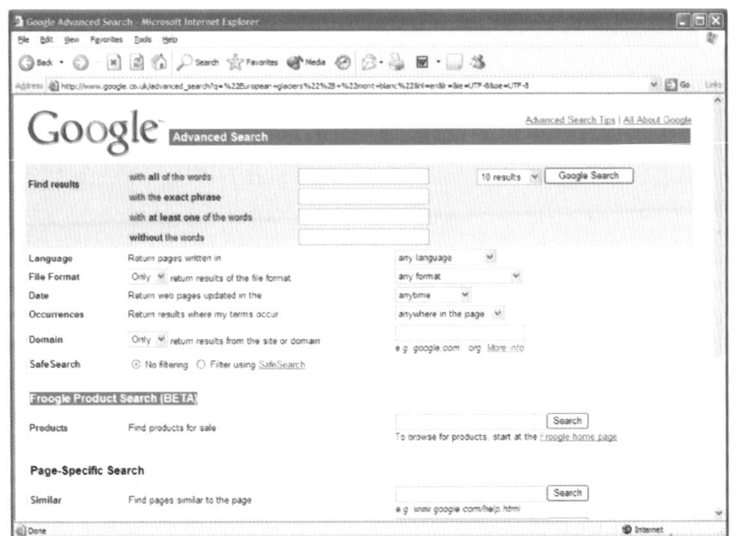

.: Using Boolean operators :.

If you try the Boolean operators, you will find they are easy to use and will save you time in the long run.

To search for two keywords, type 'AND' or '+' between them, e.g. apple and banana

To search for one keyword or another, type 'OR', e.g. apple or banana

To search for one keyword but not another, type 'NOT' or '–', e.g. apple – New York

You can combine all these operators into one search, e.g. "Big apple" – fruit + New York or NYC

PC MASTER TIP

The more information you can give the computer, the more specific the search will be and the more likely you are to find the right website.

PROGRESS CHECK EXERCISE

Can you search for a website about Cheddar cheese?

Can you find a site about Cheddar cheese and not Cheddar Gorge?

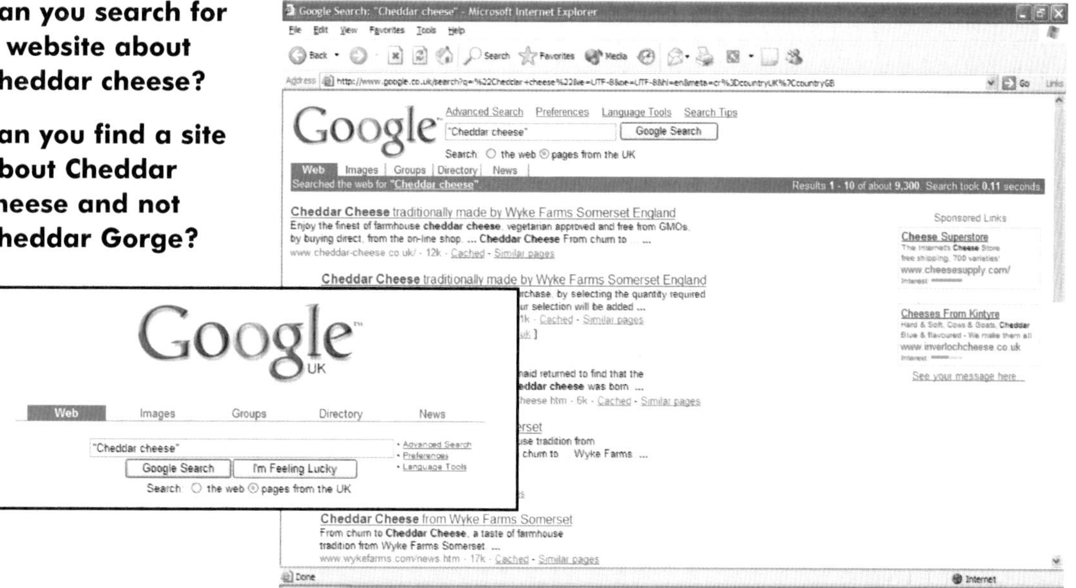

Can you use the advanced Google search to find the website for the Wimbledon Tennis Championships?

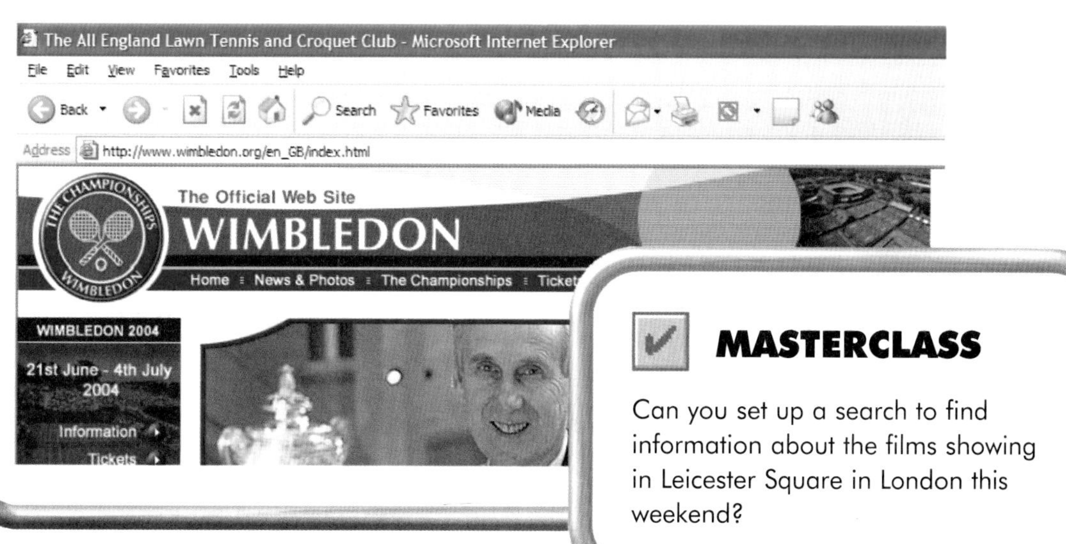

MASTERCLASS

Can you set up a search to find information about the films showing in Leicester Square in London this weekend?

AVOIDING GETTING LOST

SKILLS

.: Avoiding getting lost :.

It is easy to get distracted on the internet and to look at things that interest you rather than what you should be looking at. You might end up looking at sites that you do not need because you thought that they would be more useful than they actually are. You might also find that when you close a website, an advert pops up and you cannot get out of the loop, because when you close that one, another appears.

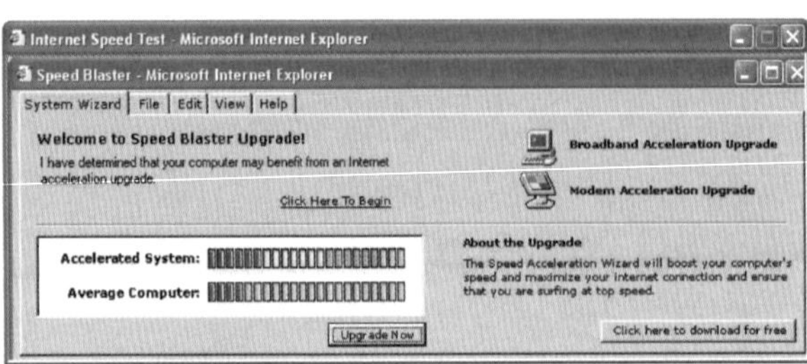

.: Stay focused! :.

You need to stay focused and although it is important to look at links from the page you are looking at, you do not always need to click on them. Sometimes you might find a link to a page that is more useful than the one you are on, but you might also open the door to a never-ending advert.

.: Stay focused! :.

Websites are written for two reasons: either because the author has an interest in the subject and wants to share it, or to make money. The way to make money on websites is to make sure that your site is a popular one. You can then sell adverts and links from your site. Some adverts are very clever and will try to 'trap' you into clicking on them by making you think that something is wrong with your computer. This is the internet equivalent of junk mail.

PC MASTER TIP

By all means follow links to other sites but unless you are just browsing to kill time, try to avoid opening unnecessary websites. A lot of time is lost on the internet by just looking for something when you should be working.

SKILL IN ACTION

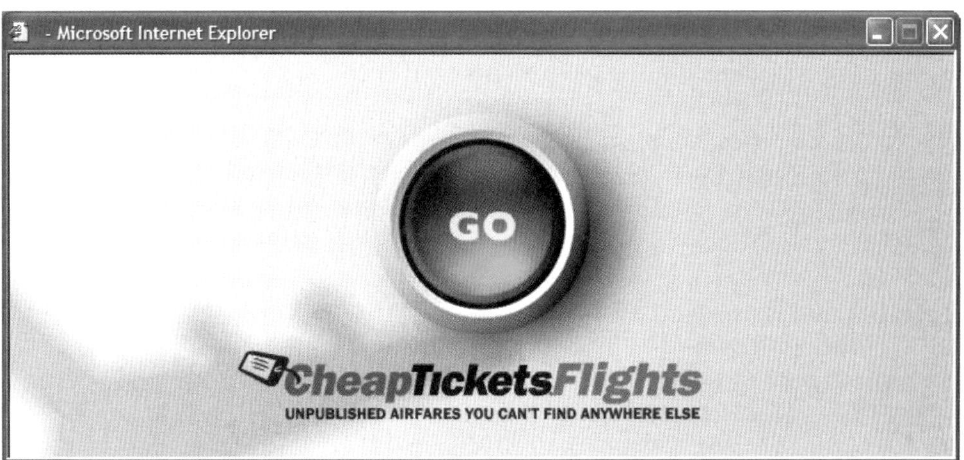

Seema the Stylist often looks on the internet for different hairstyles to use in her shop. She browses the internet but is no longer tricked into opening junk mail: she has learned her lesson!

She used to click on junk mail adverts just to see what the offers really were and would end up spending a long time going through endless websites. The offers were rarely worthwhile, so she now ignores the sites.

This means that she can get maximum benefit out of her time on the internet. She has not got broadband access at home so she pays for every minute that she is connected.

Once she has found a good site, she uses links from that site and uses the back and forward buttons to revisit old sites.

 Back 

EXERCISE

Can you spot the difference between a genuine link on a website and an advert?

SKILLS

.: Navigating the internet :.

Once you have found a suitable site for your purpose, you should try the links from that site to find other information because these have usually been found by someone to be useful. If the link is no use, click on the **back** icon to go back to the original site that you had found. If a screen pops up that is not the link or the original site, it will be an advert. If you find a site useful and go back to the original site, you can use the **forward** icon to return to it. Both these icons are on the internet toolbar.

Back

Forward

Stop

Refresh

.: Navigating icons :.

The icon with two green arrows on a white background is the **refresh** icon. This reloads a page that may have been updated or did not load properly. If you click on a link and decide that it is not what you want, press the **stop** button.

.: Adding to Favorites menu :.

If you find a really useful site that you know that you will want to visit again, select it as one of your favourites. Click on **Favorites** on the main menu and then select **Add to Favorites** from the following drop down menu:

ew Favorites Tools Help

Add to Favorites...

Organize Favorites...

Home

School

Links

PC MASTER TIP

You can keep your favourites open by clicking on the **favorites** icon on the toolbar.

PROGRESS CHECK EXERCISE

Can you follow a link by clicking on the hyperlink? Notice how the cursor changes.

Can you go back to the original page using the toolbar?

Can you spot the difference between an advert and a pop-up menu? Watch what happens to the cursor. Does it matter where you click on the image?

Can you save a page as a favourite?

MASTERCLASS

Can you organise your favourites into folders? (See pages 32–35)

SKILLS

.: Home page :.

A home page is the first web page that you see when you click on Internet Explorer. This page does not need to be on the internet, it can just be saved on your computer. Some companies do this so that there are links to relevant websites for all their staff. If this page is accessible across a network, the page and the offline links are called an intranet, as opposed to an internet. You can set up the same idea for your home computer. You can very easily choose a page that you most commonly use as your home page or you can create your own, either in HTML or using a web authoring pack.

.: Search engine home page :.

If you use the internet mainly for research, you might decide to have a search engine as your home page.

Google™ UK

Web · Images · Groups · Directory · News

Google Search | I'm Feeling Lucky

Search: the web / pages from the UK

· Advanced Search · Preferences · Language Tools

Advertise with Us - Business Solutions - Services & Tools - Jobs, Press, & Help - Go to Google.com

.: Home page :.

If you want to use the internet to find local information, you can choose a locally-based web directory.

If you want to set up your own, you can do this too.

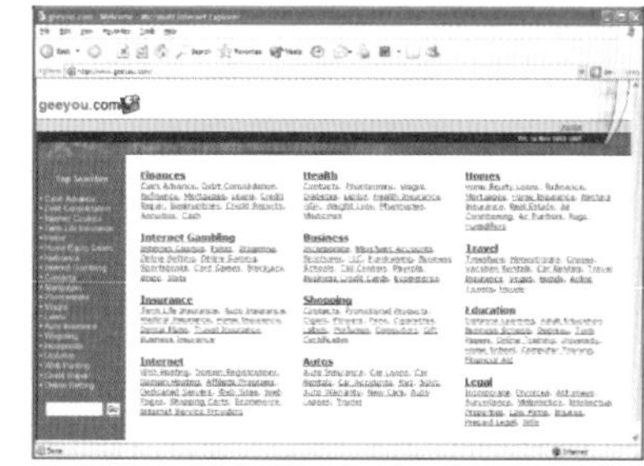

PC MASTER TIP

The idea of a home page is that it speeds up your use of the internet. It might just be a series of links that you frequently use.

 SKILL IN ACTION

Hampshire **EXPRESS**

The Times The Independent The Guardian Daily Telegraph The Sun The Star The Mirror Daily Express Daily Mail	**Latest newsflash scrolls here** Time / Date Latest story Latest sport Deadline reminders latest page designs	IT Department Stop Press News editor Sport editor Photo editor

Nick the Newspaper Editor uses a home page for his staff to access the internet. It means that they do not need to remember all the website addresses, they can just click on the links.

Nick has set up links to company-related sites on the right side of the home page and to other useful sites on the left. The users can still type in an internet address and go to different sites but they have more options that are specific to them.

Nick's home page used to be the newspaper's website, but he changed it to a search engine, altavista, before he designed his own.

This was more helpful for the other editors because they could search for information straightaway.

EXERCISE

Can you make www.altavista.co.uk your home page?

SKILLS

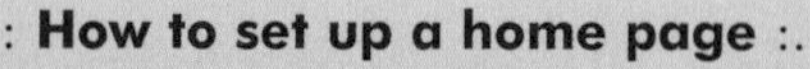

.: How to set up a home page :.

It is very easy to make a web page your home page. Once you have found a page that you like, click on **Tools** on the main menu bar.

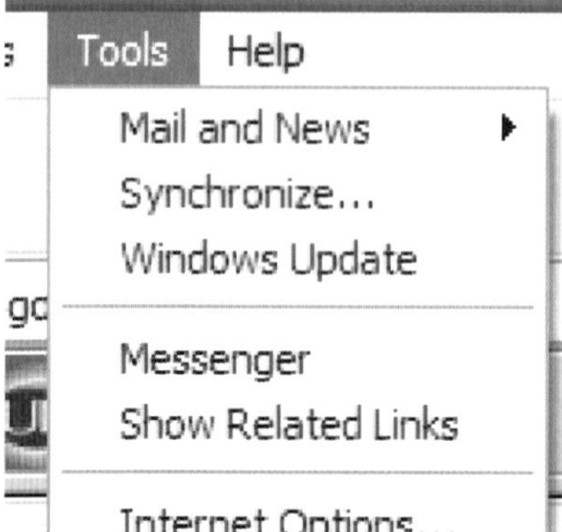

.: Internet Options :.

Select **Internet Options** to bring up the next menu.

.: Internet Options :.

Change the address in the home page box to the address of the web page you are on. Click on **Apply** then on **OK**.

If you have designed your own web page and want to make it your home page, make a note of where you saved it. Instead of writing the web address, write in the location of the file you want to use.

PC MASTER TIP

Do not select a home page with too many large images. If you are designing your own home page, do not put too many images on because they will need to load each time you open the internet and it will slow you down.

PROGRESS CHECK EXERCISE

Can you find a local web directory for your area and make it your home page?

Can you create a web page that contains links to all the websites that you usually use?

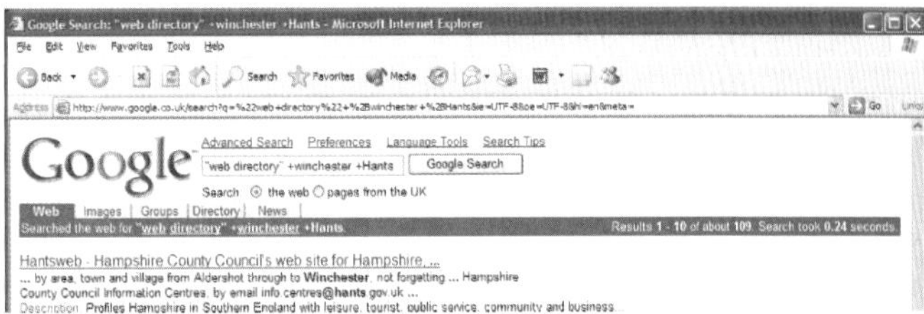

David's Homepage

My Email	Bristol City	Celebdaq	Wimbledon Tennis	Google
My Website	rubber faces	textmaker	Wey River Juniors	Ask Jeeves
Penfriend	Free txt	free clip art	freearcade	Dogpile

Can you create a home page that has lots of links to homework websites and revision sites?

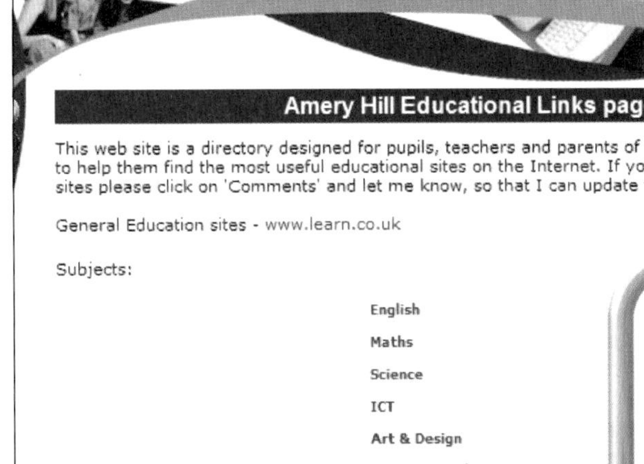

MASTERCLASS

Can you create a series of web pages that link together so that each person who uses the computer has their own home page that they can access by clicking on their name?

ELIABILITY OF WEBSITES

SKILLS

.: Government sites :.

There are millions of websites. They all give information but there is no guarantee that the information is correct. There is no regulatory body that monitors the internet and checks that what is available is up-to-date and accurate. A useful skill therefore is to know how much you can trust the site before you spend too long reading it. Anybody can create a website and they can put anything that they want on the site as long as it does not break any decency laws. The police are able to find out who runs websites by using the web provider's records.

The site below is probably reliable because it is a government website. You can tell this from the ending of the web address, e.g. gov.uk.

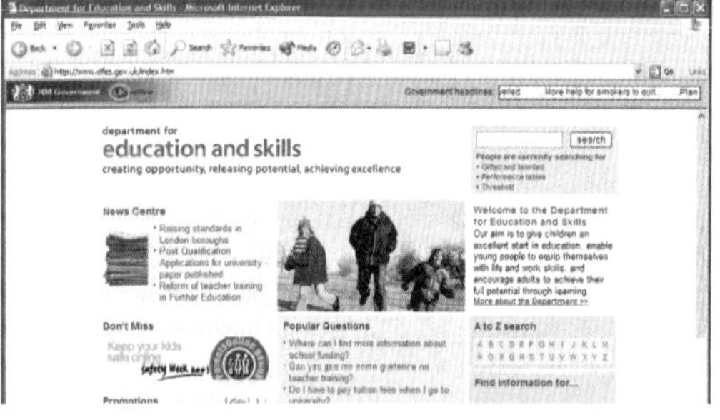

.: Official sites :.

Official websites are more likely to be correct. An official website will have the backing of whoever or whatever the article is about. Information on these sites is likely to be reliable.

Other things to look at are the links to and from the site. Are they from good sources or do they link to similar sites of dubious reliability? Some sites are sponsored. Are the sponsors reliable? Are they just a collection of adverts? All these factors can help you judge the reliability of the site and its author.

PC MASTER TIP

Remember, anyone can write a website. Do not believe everything that you read without checking it.

SKILL IN ACTION

Sophie the Student needs to be very careful to check that any information that she gets from the internet is correct. She spends a lot of time looking at websites to decide whether they are reliable or not. This is important, whether she is finding information for research, or for her social life.

It is obvious that the information for her projects needs to be correct, but it is also important that any other information she reads on the internet is checked as well. If she is feeling unwell, she can look on the internet to see what the symptoms might indicate. She should still see a doctor, because the site could have been written by an unqualified person.

Also, she might have misread what her symptoms mean.

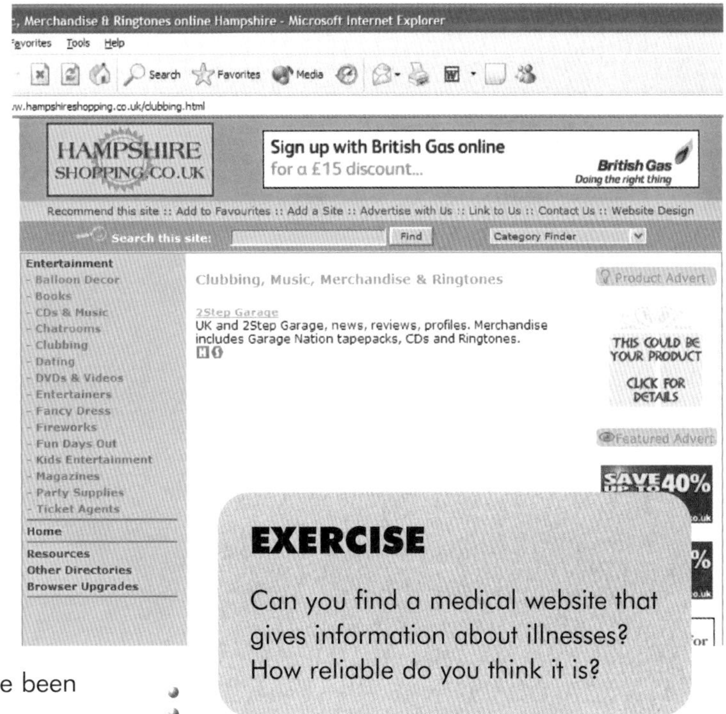

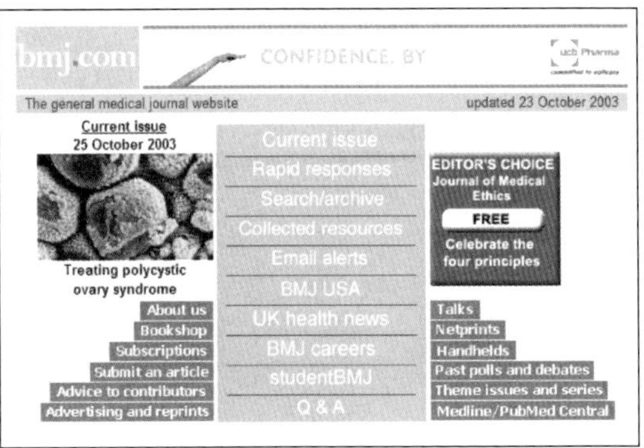

EXERCISE

Can you find a medical website that gives information about illnesses? How reliable do you think it is?

SKILLS

.: Checking a URL :.

The first thing to look at is the Universal Resource Locator (URL) or web address of the website. The ending of the address will tell you a lot about who runs a website. If you are looking for information, a site with the ending gov.uk will be a government website, police.uk will be an official police site and ac.uk or sch.uk will be an academic establishment.

.: Checking a URL :.

If you look at the URL and are not sure that it is an official website, this does not necessarily mean that it is unreliable. Look at some of the links from the website, where do they go to? Do these sites have more recognisable URLs?

.: Reliability of internet sites :.

One other way to check for reliability is to look at who has sponsored the website and who advertises on the site. If the adverts are for companies that are linked to the site, it is more likely to be reliable as they have paid to advertise to their target audience. If the adverts are general, they are sold centrally to the webspace providers and advertised on all their sites. This will not help you judge the reliability of the site.

PC MASTER TIP

Look at two or three sites to check trivial information. However, if you are looking for important information, e.g. about money or medical matters, you should check with a professional before taking advice from the internet.

PROGRESS CHECK EXERCISE

Can you find a reliable site to find out about traffic news? One element of reliability here will be how up-to-date it is.

Can you find a reliable news website? Try to find a less reliable news website.

Can you find some tour dates for a band touring this year? How do you know if they are correct?

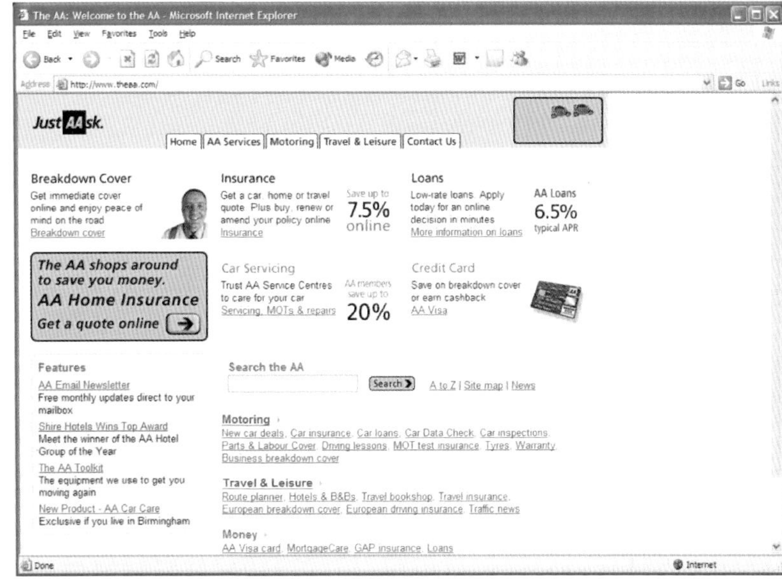

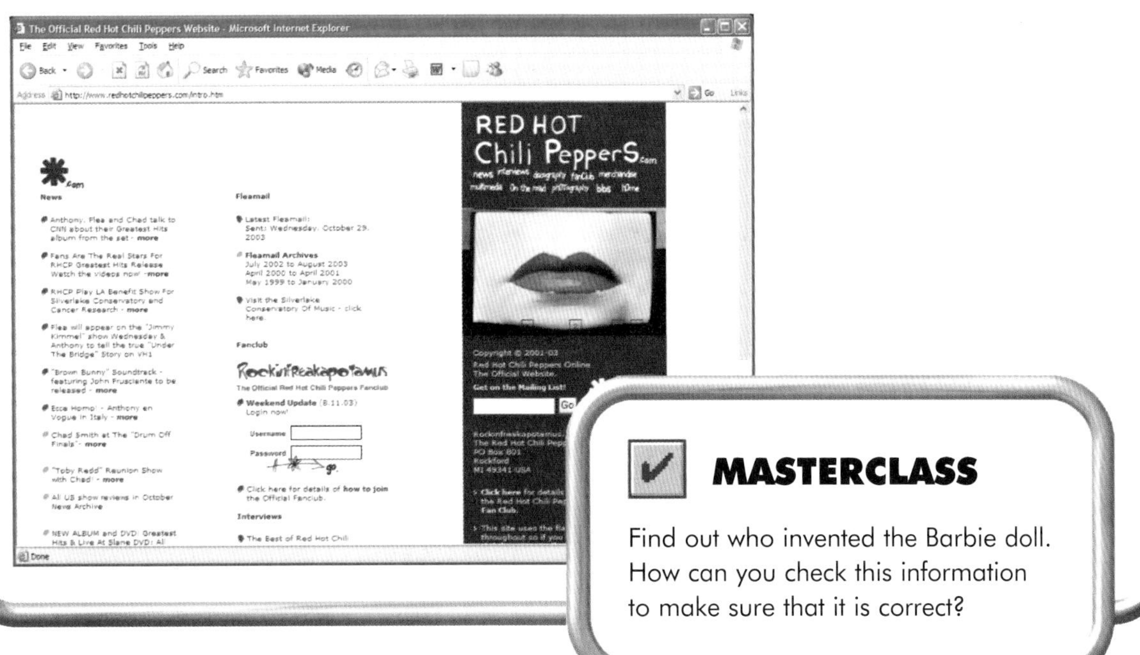

MASTERCLASS

Find out who invented the Barbie doll. How can you check this information to make sure that it is correct?

PURPOSE OF A WEBSITE

SKILLS

.: Website design :.

When designing a website, it is very important to consider what you are trying to achieve. This will not only affect the style and layout of the page but will also affect the language that you use. Do you want to give information, do you want to try to persuade someone to do something or do you want to describe something that you have seen or read?

A persuasive website will need to be eye-catching and should try to encourage the reader to be interested in what you have to offer. One website that tries to advertise and persuade at the same time is amazon.co.uk. The site advertises new offers on the introduction page.

Their database records your past purchases and advises you of other products that you might like to try. There are also reviews of products for sale.

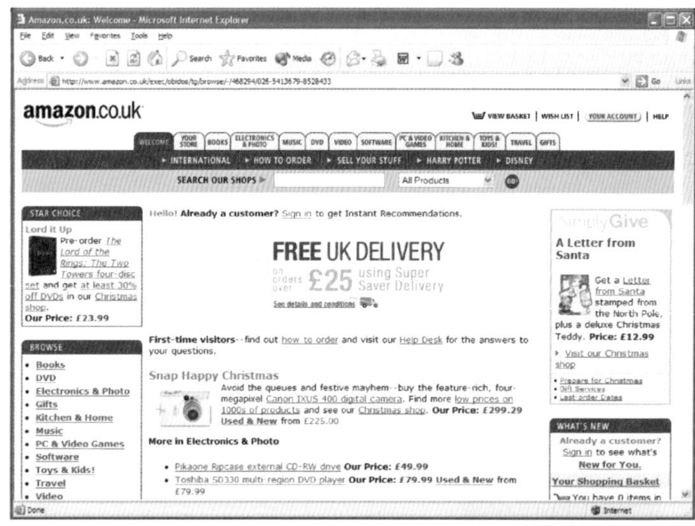

.: Website design :.

If you are trying to give information, people who are interested will probably read it anyway, so it is important to make the site as easy to use as possible.

Large pictures will take a long time to show on the screens of slower computers so if they are not necessary, do not use them.

PC MASTER TIP

Your audience will expect the website to reflect its purpose. Make sure your website follows a suitable style.

SKILL IN ACTION

Harry the Hotelier looked at lots of other websites before he started to write his own. He checked the style of the others and got ideas about what to include. Most hotel websites have a photo of the hotel and the contact details on the introduction page, with a list of links either down the side or at the bottom.

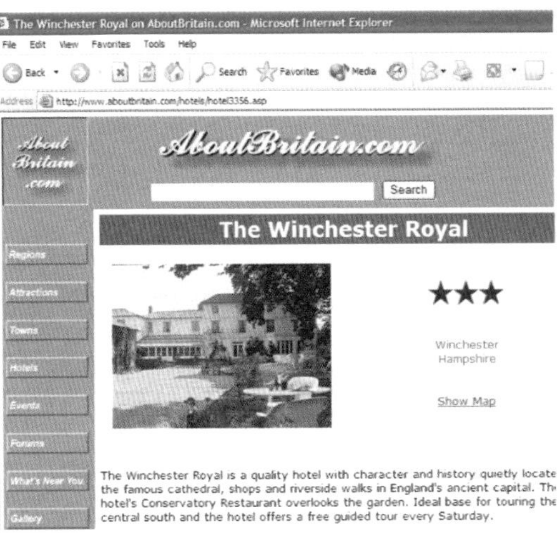

Harry then made a list of things that he wanted the website to do:

- Advertise the hotel
- Persuade people coming to the area to stay at the hotel
- Describe the hotel and its facilities
- Give examples of things to do in the area and link to their sites
- Describe how to find the hotel
- Provide an online booking service.

Having made the purpose of the site clear, Harry needs to plan the pages. He wants an introduction page and links to a page about the facilities and the rooms. He also wants to link to a booking page, a directions page and to other local websites.

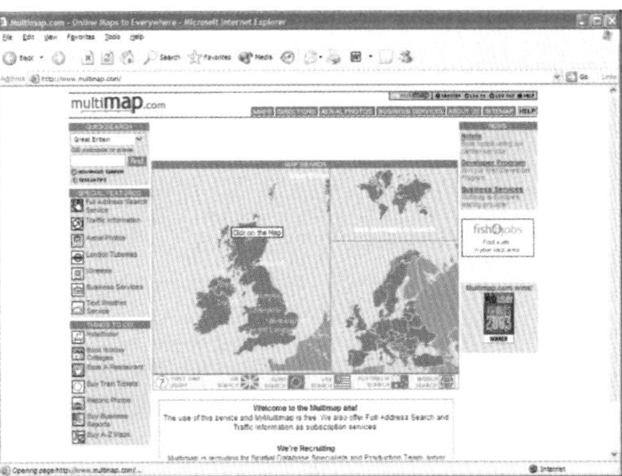

This shows a website on the internet that provides maps.

EXERCISE

Look at five different hotel websites. What makes the best site better than all the others? Make a list of the things that are common to all five sites.

SKILLS

.: Target audience :.

The first thing to do is to decide on your target audience. Who do you want to read the website? You need to think about your audience, for example if you are targeting children, the site should be:

- colourful
- have large titles
- contain more pictures than text
- have moving images.

If you are producing a professional site, it will need to:

- follow the corporate style
- look business-like and formal
- contain relevant pictures.

Once you have decided on the audience, you will need to look at the style of text and think about how to construct the page to best meet their expectations.

.: Purpose of work :.

Before you start writing, you should think about what your website is trying to achieve. Are you trying to sell something? Are you giving information? Are you trying to entertain the reader? Whatever the purpose, this will affect the way you write your website. Most school websites are written to inform:

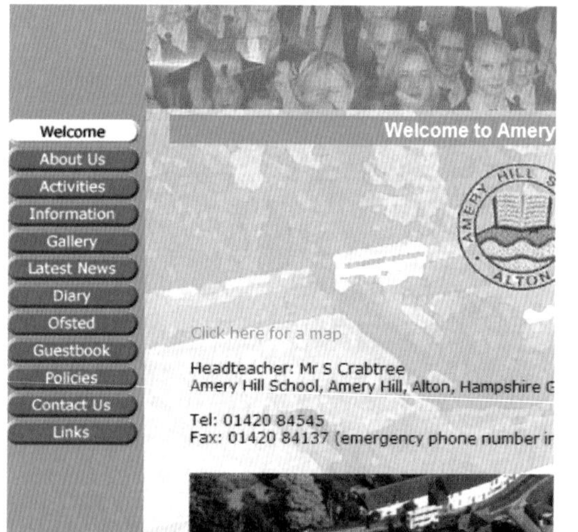

 PC MASTER TIP

Web pages that describe or explain should have more text than those that entertain or persuade. Websites that entertain should include more white space to break up the text and make it easier to read.

PROGRESS CHECK EXERCISE

Can you design a web page to appeal to children, e.g. about a new toy?

Make a list of points that you would need to consider.

You have been asked to build a website for an entertainer at children's parties.

Who would your target audience be? How would you design your work to meet their expectations? Consider these points:

- The age group of the audience
- The number of pages
- Colours
- The size and style of font
- What it needs to say.
- What the most important information on the page is going to be.

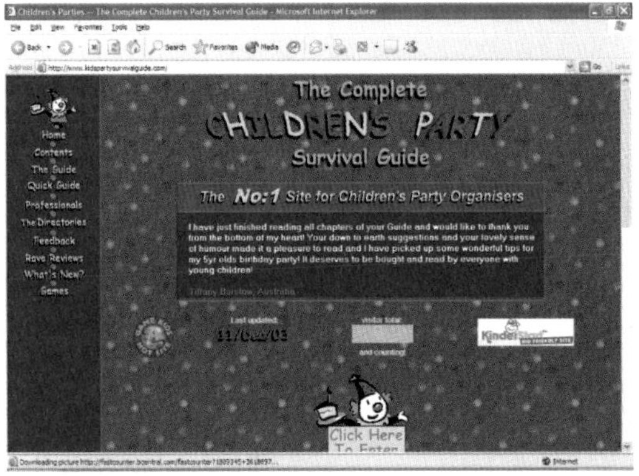

You have decided to write a website about books you have read. How will this web page differ from the children's party page?

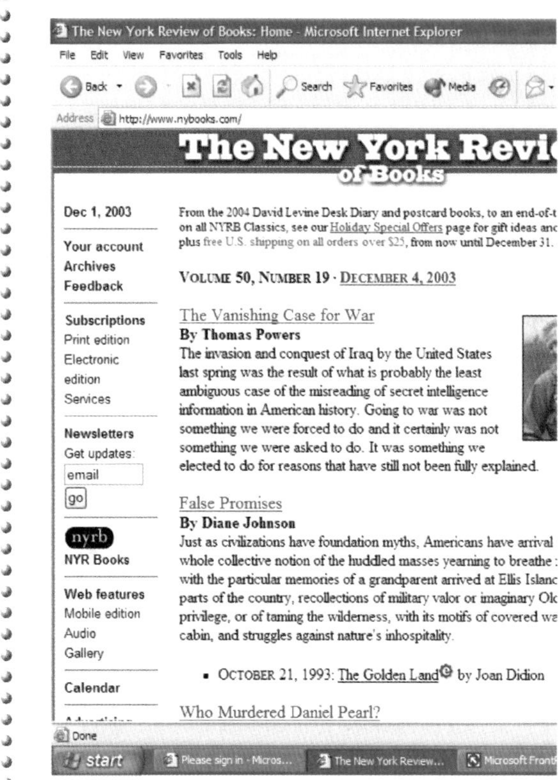

MASTERCLASS

Your local community centre has asked you to design a website for them. What must you include in your website?

SKILLS

.: Web authoring software :.

If you want to create a web page and do not want the job of learning HTML, you could buy some web authoring software. One example of this is Microsoft® FrontPage. It is a very simple program to use. The page is created in the same way as it would be in a word processor and the program will write the HTML for you.

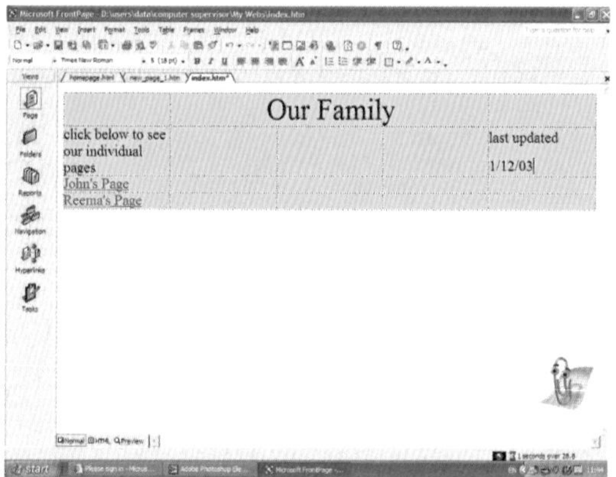

.: Web authoring software :.

Using one of these programs is another good way to learn HTML as you can see the language after you have created the page.

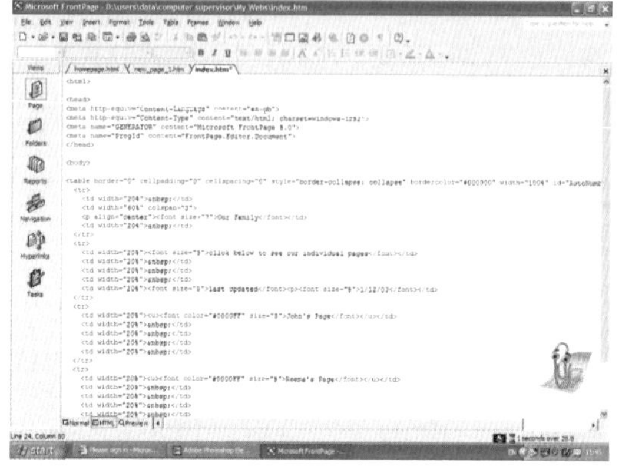

.: A website navigation tree :.

You can create any number of pages using FrontPage and you can set up links between them. Even if you are not going to put the page on the internet, it will look like a complete website. You can see the structure of the site by looking at the navigation tree.

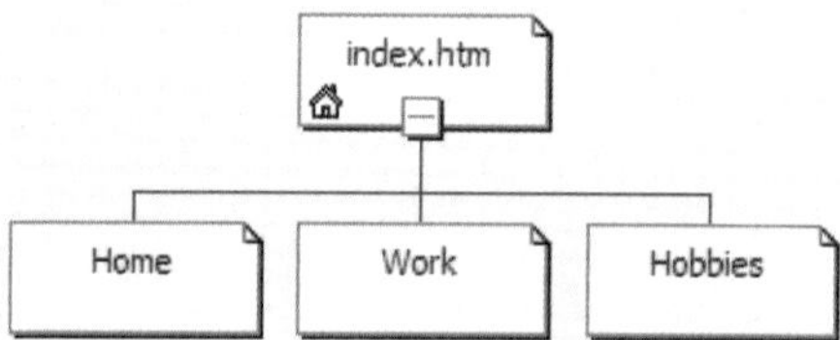

PC MASTER TIP

There are lots of different types of web authoring programs. They vary dramatically in price. Look at some demonstration versions and see what you like using most before you buy.

SKILL IN ACTION

Hotel Royal Homepage

- Click here to email reception
- Click here to book a table in the Renaissance restaurant
- Click here to view your tab
- Click here to book a wake up call
- Click here to order a film
- Click here to access the internet
- Click here for local information
- Click here for local taxi companies

Harry the Hotelier writes his website in FrontPage because he is used to Microsoft® products and understands how they work. He also has an intranet in the hotel with information about the hotel, services and local information. All his customers have access to this intranet.

It is easy for Harry to update the site because he can simply access the files from his main computer and change them. Once he has saved them, they are updated on every computer on the network.

Harry started off with a simple web page which linked to times for breakfast, the evening meals and checkout times. As customers asked new questions and came up with suggestions, the site grew and grew.

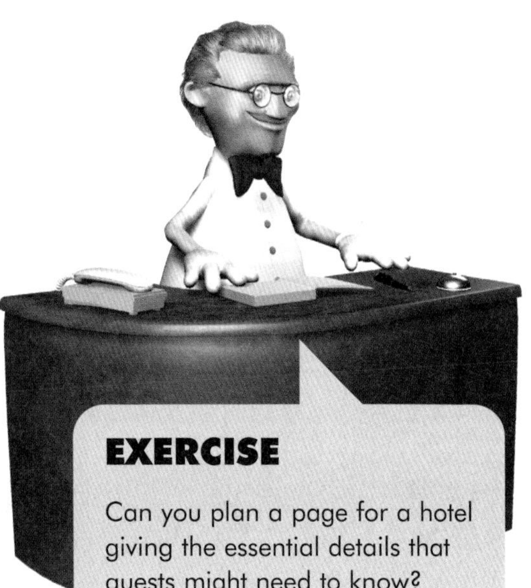

EXERCISE

Can you plan a page for a hotel giving the essential details that guests might need to know?

SKILLS

.: Planning a web page :.

The secret to making a web page is to plan it carefully first. It is best to start off with a table so that the page is already broken up into sections. You can then easily insert an image on the right-hand side of the page by putting it in a box on the right-hand side.

.: Make the tables invisible :.

Change the font size and colour to make the page look the way you want. Make sure that the table has no borders so that it becomes invisible.

.: Removing borders :.

To remove the borders, select **Table** from the main menu bar and then select **Properties**. Change the size of the border to 0.

.: Using Preview :.

If you want to see how the page looks, click on the **Preview** tab towards the bottom left of the page. If you click on **HTML**, you can see the language. This is what you would have to write if you were using Notepad instead of FrontPage.

.: Adding a hyperlink :.

To add a hyperlink, select the word that will be used as the link and use the **Hyperlink** button. Choose where to link the word to.

PC MASTER TIP

Keep the structure of the site as simple as possible. Do not forget to create links back to the main menu page from every page.

PROGRESS CHECK EXERCISE

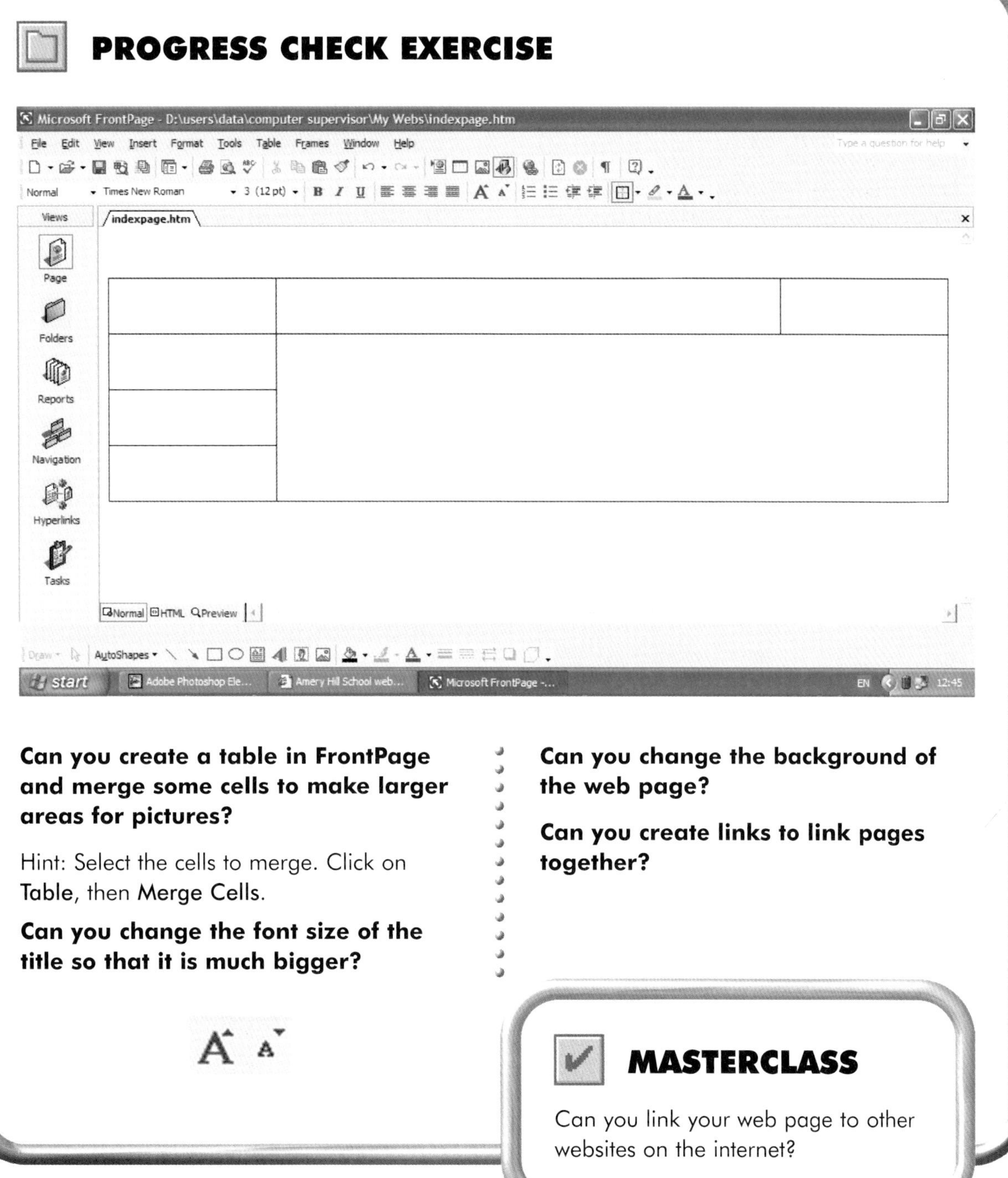

Can you create a table in FrontPage and merge some cells to make larger areas for pictures?

Hint: Select the cells to merge. Click on Table, then Merge Cells.

Can you change the font size of the title so that it is much bigger?

Can you change the background of the web page?

Can you create links to link pages together?

MASTERCLASS

Can you link your web page to other websites on the internet?

SKILLS

.: Safe internet use :.

The internet is a very useful tool but it can be used for illegal and improper activities. No one should be afraid to use the internet, but you should be aware of some of the problems that can occur.

.: Chatrooms :.

The number of reported incidents of abuse over the internet has increased over the last few years. One of the biggest problems arises with chatrooms. A chatroom is an area where people can join in the chat and send messages to each other in real time. The problem with chatrooms is that you do not really know who you are talking to.

Chatrooms exist because, when used properly, they are great for groups of similar minded people to get together and discuss things. Just be aware that the person you are talking to may not be who you think they are.

.: Safe internet use :.

Another problem is fraud. It is possible for people to obtain your credit card number or bank details over the internet and then use your money to buy themselves things. You need to be very careful who you give these details to. **Never** email this information to anyone.

.: Safe internet use :.

Be careful how much information you put on a website. Schools and youth groups are advised not to put photographs of pupils and their names together on the internet. There should not be any close-up images. Be aware that if you put your address on the web, people can find you.

PC MASTER TIP

Do not give out personal details on the internet unless you are absolutely sure that the receiver is a trusted and reliable company or person and that they can keep the information secure.

SKILL IN ACTION

Donald the Doctor wanted a web page about his family so that his parents in Africa could see all the latest news and photographs. His children want to be able to chat to their cousins in Africa.

Donald looked into this and decided on the best way to do it. He knew that he was going to write the web page using Microsoft® FrontPage and that he had some free webspace with his internet service provider. He just needed to decide what information to put on the site. He did not want any of his patients to have access to his personal details. He also wanted to keep his children safe from possible abuse in chatrooms.

Donald agreed with the family what they should do. He already had some software on the computer that blocks inappropriate websites and he decided that the children were not allowed to use chatrooms at all. They could use MSN messenger instead.

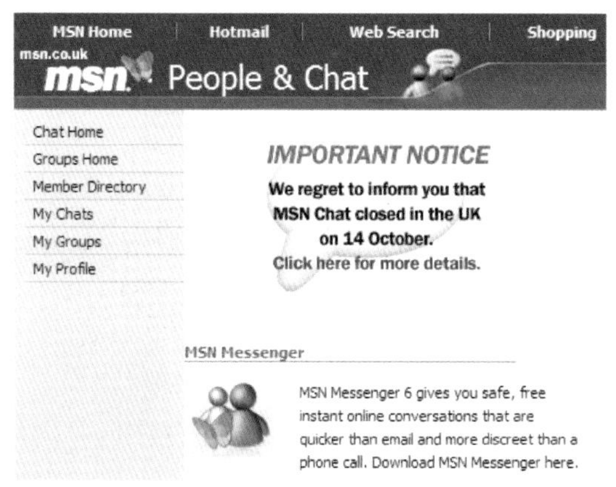

This is a real time conversation but you can only chat to people if you know their email address. Donald was happy that this was safe as long as the children were careful who they allowed to enter the chat. It was also agreed that there was no need to put surnames, their address or telephone number on the website.

The family decided that they would have a calendar of dates for birthdays, etc. They would include photographs because as there were no other personal details, there should be no danger to the children. They would have to give the website address to their relations as it would be difficult to find by searching.

EXERCISE

If you were to write a website about yourself, what information would you leave out in order to protect yourself?

SKILLS

.: Content Advisor :.

There are safety measures available on your computer. You can change the internet settings so that a lot of information is filtered out. This is done by right clicking on the **Internet Explorer** icon and selecting **Internet Options**. Choose the **Content** tab. One of the options is the **Content Advisor**. Select this and the following menu appears:

.: Internet security software :.

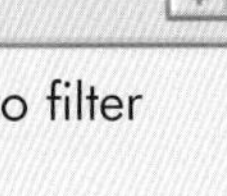

You can also buy software that allows you to filter information so that children cannot access inappropriate material on the internet. This will help to prevent them from seeing anything that they should not, but you need to keep it up-to-date.

Anyone using the internet should be aware of the dangers of chatrooms. There are other alternatives to chatrooms that only allow you to speak to those whose email address you know. You can also set up your email software so that you only receive emails from people whose address is in your address book.

Never give details of bank accounts or credit cards to any company that you are not directly dealing with and have not got a telephone contact for. Never deal with companies that cannot guarantee the security of any data that you send them. This usually involves something called a 'secure server'. The company should give you an account number or password which will mean that you do not have to send the details again.

Try to keep your passwords safe from others, do not write them down. Remember to change them regularly. Most banks now ask only for certain letters from your password so that there is less danger of someone seeing your password as you type it.

PC MASTER TIP

If in doubt about anything, do not do it. If your details get into the wrong hands, you can regard them as being in the public domain for all to see. The majority of people will not abuse the information but some might and that is what you need to be aware of.

PROGRESS CHECK EXERCISE

Can you think of a good series of passwords that would be hard to guess?

Try to use a combination of numbers and letters.

Make a list of things that you should not put on the internet.

Give it to the rest of your family so that they understand what they can and cannot do.

Can you set up a web-based email address without giving any personal details?

Make a list of the pros and cons of shopping online and decide whether you would consider doing it.

Make a list of the pros and cons of online banking to try to persuade a member of your family that you should (or should not) be able to set up an account.

MASTERCLASS

Can you set up your internet access so that there is very little chance of inappropriate material being accessed?

INDEX

1010010010101101001010010111010010101011101010110111000010